Introduction

Part 1: The Basics of Elite Gourmet Bread Machine

When I was a tiny young lady, I saw my mother heat new bread for the family from time to time. A similar love for bread making gradually moved to me, and presently I try to treat my children with delectable bread exactly how my mother did.

Initially, I used to heat the bread in a broiler, yet it didn't actually turn out how I would have preferred it to. Thus, I pondered changing to a bread creator. That is the point at which my better half skilled me the Elite Gourmet Bread Machine on our wedding commemoration. I was unable to be happier!

This machine is minimal, lightweight, and incredibly valuable with regards to making various kinds of bread. It totally changed my bread making experience since it accompanies probably the most astounding capacities. I love testing in the kitchen, and trust me, this apparatus is ideally suited for any individual who is an enthusiastic bread producer! All things considered, saying that this apparatus has made my life much more straightforward would definitely be an understatement.

Therefore, remembering that, I considered offering my experience to you all.

Apart from that, you will likewise observe all the vital data with regards to its determinations, capacities, and features.

What's more, I have additionally expounded on a portion of the frill that I coexisted with this machine. Thus, without burning through any additional time, give this cookbook a read!

Key Specifications

The Elite Gourmet Bread Machine is planned from non-harmful and solid material. Because of its simplicity of dealing with, this bread producer can be utilized by an amateur too. In this segment, I will talk about a portion of the vital details of Elite Gourmet's bread machine.

LCD Display

With the assistance of the LCD show, everything is obviously demonstrated. You can choose the ideal capacity and press start. The rest will effortlessly be dealt with by the Elite Gourmet Bread Machine in only a couple minutes!

Removable and Non-stick Bread Pan

The bread container of Elite Gourmet Bread Machine can be eliminated from the apparatus. Likewise, it additionally includes a non-stick covering, which makes it simple to clean. At the point when you eliminate the dish from the machine, it gives you the opportunity to clean the inside without making a great deal of mess.

Removable Kneading Paddle

After eliminating the bread from the container, you may see that there are monstrous imprints from the manipulating paddle. While this little part inside the skillet can assist you with shaping a reliable player, it can likewise be a cause of irritation. Along these lines, with regards to baking your most loved bread in Elite Gourmet, you can keep this stress to the side! It permits you to eliminate the plying paddle once its task is finished, and can partake in a sans spot bread.

Convection Cooking

With the assistance of the convection cooking, the hotness inside the apparatus gets flowed equally. The Elite Gourmet Bread Machine likewise works similarly and ensures that nothing is left uncooked. In addition, it likewise assists with preparing the food quickly.

Main Functions

Baking portions of bread with Elite Gourmet Bread Machine is super-simple and guarantees that you never become weary of testing. You just need to follow these means referenced below:

- Add ingredients
- Select the cycle
- Press start

See simple! This programmable machine gives you the choice to browse three portion sizes and nineteen baking capacities. Take a look!

Basic

Here is the simplest method for baking bread that everybody loves! With the fundamental capacity, you can without much of a stretch prepare the standard white bread and relish it with jam or butter.

Quick

The speedy menu will assist you with baking your bread significantly quicker than the typical time. It is on the grounds that this capacity doesn't need the utilization of yeast. Hence, to trust that an extensive stretch will make sound bread for your family, this is the right option!

Sweet

The sweet setting on Elite Gourmet Bread Machine will assist you with baking delicate and cushy bread. It is normally loaded up with jam or cream cheddar, which makes it ideal for a treat thought. All things considered, this specific capacity is my favorite!

French

French bread is longer and smaller than normal bread. Likewise, it is additionally hard and dried up outwardly and has a delicate and light piece. Need to give your hands a shot this formula? Indeed, the Elite Gourmet Bread Maker is available to you! By choosing its French capacity, you can prepare a dried up portion of bread very much like the first recipe!

Whole wheat

To make one of the best bread plans, you don't need to search for a different machine. The bread producer from Elite Gourmet has a choice to heat entire wheat bread. Simply add exceptional bread flour and a smidgen of honey.

Rye

The rye bread is more obscure and denser when contrasted with the fundamental and entire wheat bread. Likewise, it includes less gluten than standard flour bread. Accordingly, for a natural taste, you can pick the rye function.

Gluten-Free

Individuals who are gluten and dairy prejudiced can make sans gluten bread by pushing on this capacity. In addition to the fact that it is really sound, yet it additionally tastes better compared to ordinary without gluten bread.

Rice Bread

While making this kind of bread, you use rice flour rather than wheat flour. Rice bread is an extraordinary substitute for without gluten bread and won't make responses individuals who are gluten-intolerant.

Sandwich

Sandwich bread is arranged explicitly for sandwiches. Therefore, in the event that your children are in the mind-set to eat a yummy treat, you know what to do!

Cake

With the assistance of this capacity, you can blend the cake hitter without tiring your arms. Simply pour every one of the fixings and press the cake work, and your hitter will be prepared inside minutes!

Wholemeal Dough

The wholemeal batter is made utilizing the wheat bit. It helps in adding flavor and nourishment to prepared items, explicitly bread.

Pizza Dough

Pizza batter can be produced using scratch utilizing the Elite Gourmet Bread Machine. Add flour, yeast, water, olive oil, and put them in the bread dish. Select the Pizza Dough capacity and make a yummy treat inside a couple minutes.

Leaven Dough

Leaven batter is utilized for baking raised bread. It contains baking yeast, baking pop/powder. These fixings make the batter rise and make a light item. The Leaven Dough work gives you the ideal mixture to make light and vaporous bread.

Knead

Kneading is the method involved with making batter for bread. It requires an individual to blend the fixings, like flour and water, to reinforce the end result utilizing their hands. In this manner, to save you from investing some part of energy, essentially put these fixings into the bread container and select the ideal function.

Mix

The blend work in Elite Gourmet Bread Machine assists you with blending the elements of a bread with consistency.

Jam

Want to make stick at home? Indeed, you got this! The Elite Gourmet Bread Machine accompanies an in-fabricated jam-production work, which will assist you with appreciating hand crafted jam easily. From strawberries to apples, you can put any kind of natural product inside the bread dish and add granulated sugar, lemon juice, and gelatin. Select the jam capacity and trust that the clock will stop. Empty the blend into a container and keep it in the refrigerator after it gets cool.

Yogurt

Yogurt is one of my cherished dairy items that fill my belly in only two or three spoons. As a rule, I incline toward making yogurt at home, and this awesome kitchen apparatus has made it even more helpful for me!

The interaction is basic. Add the necessary measure of milk to the container, and afterward pour in some yogurt. Close the top and press the yogurt choice. In the following not many hours, you can appreciate the yummy natively constructed yogurt!

Defrost

This choice ensures that you don't squander the extra bread that sits on the edge of your fridge. Take out as many cuts from the cooler and spot them inside the skillet. Presently select the thaw out choice from the menu. The cuts of the bread will taste new, and you will not need to squander any food.

Essential Features

Now that I have clarified the critical determinations and the various elements of the Elite Gourmet Bread Machine, it's time we move to another part. Here, I will discuss every one of the fundamental elements of this lightweight and super-practical bread producer. So, moving along, we should simply plunge straight into the features.

Delay Start Function

Most of the time, bread machines accompany a postponed start clock. This capacity permits you to add all the bread fixings and set a clock. After the clock is finished, the machine turns all alone. Typically, it is done expedite with the goal that you can appreciate new bread right when you awaken. That, yet you can set it in the first part of the day and return home to newly heated bread.

The Elite Gourmet Bread Machine accompanies a 15-hour defer time. Thusly, you get newly heated bread the second you need to eat it.

Indicator Light

This bread producer by Elite Gourmet accompanies pointer light.
It tells you precisely when your food is ready.

Viewing Window

The review window on Elite Gourmet Bread Machine allows you to check whether your food is getting cooked appropriately or not. It is on top of the lid.

Cool-Touch Exterior

The outside of this machine stays cool even subsequent to cooking your beloved sort of bread. This guarantees that you don't wear your hand while removing the bread from the appliance.

Keep Warm Setting

Even after the food is prepared, you can keep it inside the bread creator. The Keep Warm Setting ensures that the food stays warm for around 60 minutes.

Anti-slip Silicone Feet

The bread-production machine highlights hostile to slip silicone feet, which keeps it from tumbling from the counter.

Package Included

Apart from the Elite Gourmet Bread Machine, you will track down a few adornments in the bundle. These will assist you with making the baking system significantly simpler. Investigate every one of the things that accompany this great cooking appliance.

Measuring cup

An estimating cup will ensure that you don't wreck the estimations of the fixings that go in a specific food. There are minuscule markings on the external surface of the cup, with the assistance of which you can sort out the specific measure of stuff that goes in the bread pan.

Bread pan

The bread container of Elite Gourmet Bread Machine is produced using non-stick material, which makes it simple to clean. Aside from that, it likewise can be eliminated from the machine easily, which helps in the comprehensive cleaning.

Measuring spoon

An estimating spoon assists you with estimating how much a fixing. The fixing can either be fluid, or it tends to be dry. With the Elite Gourmet Bread Machine, you get an estimating spoon that can be utilized to place each fixing in the ideal quantity.

Metal snare to lift the plying paddle

This adornment is utilized to lift the manipulating paddle from the bread dish easily. Subsequently, you will not need to invest some parcel of energy while eliminating it from the pan.

Kneading blade

The manipulating edge helps blend every one of the fixings to frame a strong hitter, which can be subsequently used to prepare various sorts of bread. The most amazing aspect of this edge is that it very well may be taken out from the bread dish. It ensures that your bread comes out generally overall quite clean with next to no deformity.

Chapter 2: Basic Breads
Sourdough Bread
Serves 12

Sourdough Starter:
1½ teaspoons speedy dynamic
dry yeast 4 cups warm water
3 cups universally
handy flour 4
teaspoons sugar
Bread:
½ cup water
3 cups bread
flour 2
tablespoons
sugar 1½
teaspoons salt

1 teaspoon fast dynamic dry yeast

1. Prepare the sourdough starter somewhere around multi week prior to baking the bread by dissolving 1½ teaspoons yeast in warm water in a glass bowl.
2. Stir in 3 cups flour and the 4 teaspoons sugar. Beat with electric blender on medium speed for 1 moment or until smooth.
3. Cover freely and let remain at room temperature for multi week or until combination is effervescent and has a sharp fragrance; when prepared, cover tight and refrigerate until prepared to use.
4. When you are prepared to heat the bread, measure out 1 cup of the sourdough starter and all of the leftover bread fixings cautiously, setting in bread machine container the wet fixings first, then, at that point, dry ingredients.
5. Select Basic and Medium Crust, then, at that point, press Start.
6. Remove prepared bread from dish and cool on a wire rack.

1 cup warm water
2 tablespoons agave nectar
¼ cup fruit purée
3 cups bread flour
1 teaspoon salt
2¼ teaspoons fast ascent yeast

1. Add fluid fixings to the bread pan.
2. Measure and add dry fixings (aside from yeast) to the bread pan.
3. Make a well in the focal point of the dry fixings and add the yeast.
4. Snap the baking skillet into the bread machine and close the lid.
5. Choose the Basic cycle, favored outside shading and press Start.
6. Remove and permit to cool on a wire rack when heated, before serving.

4½ cups 100 percent entire wheat flour
1½ cups warm

water

⅓ cup olive oil

⅓ cup honey

2 teaspoons salt

1 tablespoon dynamic dry yeast

1. Add water to the bread machine.
2. Measure and add the oil first, then, at that point, the honey in a similar estimating cup: this will make the honey get out of the estimating cup more easily.
3. Add salt, then, at that point, flour.
4. Make a little well in the flour and add the yeast.
5. Set to Wheat Bread cycle, pick hull tone, and press Start.
6. Remove and permit to cool on a wire rack when heated, before serving.

1 cup water

1½ teaspoons salt

2 tablespoons sugar

1 tablespoon butter

2 teaspoons caraway seed

2 cups bread flour

1 cup rye flour

1½ teaspoons fast dynamic yeast

1. Place every one of the fixings with the exception of yeast in the bread machine container in the request listed.
2. Make a well in the focal point of the dry fixings and add the yeast.
3. Choose the Basic cycle for 1½-pound (680-g) portion and medium outside layer tone. Press Start.
4. Remove bread when done and permit to cool for 10 minutes prior to cutting with a bread knife.

¾ cup water

⅔ cup moment pureed

potatoes 1 egg
2 tablespoons margarine,
unsalted 2 tablespoons
white sugar
¼ cup dry milk
powder 1 teaspoon
salt
3 cups bread flour
1½ teaspoons dynamic dry yeast

1. Add the fixings to bread machine in the request recorded previously. Save yeast for next step.
2. Make a well in the focal point of the dry fixings and add the yeast.
3. Press the Basic cycle, pick light to medium outside layer tone, and press Start.
4. Remove from bread dish and permit to cool on a wire rack before serving.

1¼ cups tepid water
¼ cup molasses
2 tablespoons unsweetened cocoa
powder 1 teaspoon ocean salt
1 cup entire wheat
flour 1 cup rye flour
2 cups unbleached universally
handy flour 2½ tablespoons
vegetable oil
1½ tablespoons stuffed earthy
colored sugar 1 tablespoon
caraway seeds
2½ teaspoons moment yeast

1. Note: all fixings ought to be at room temperature before baking.
2. Add each of the fixings in the request recorded above, holding

yeast.
3. Make a well in the focal point of the dry fixings and add the yeast.
4. Set the bread machine on Whole Wheat cycle, select hull tone, and press Start.
5. Remove and let the portion cool for 15 minutes before slicing.

2¼ cups entire wheat flour

¾ cup ground oatmeal

2 tablespoons wheat bran

2 tablespoons flaxseed meal

2 tablespoons indispensable wheat gluten 1 tablespoon batter enhancer

1 teaspoon salt

2⅔ teaspoons dynamic dry yeast 2 tablespoons olive oil

1 tablespoon agave nectar 1 tablespoon brown sugar

1 cup warm water (marginally hotter than room temperature)

1. Set the yeast to the side and join the excess dry fixings in a blending bowl.
2. Add the fluids to the bread machine first, trailed by the dry ingredients.
3. Make a little well in the flour and add the yeast.
4. Press Whole Wheat cycle, light covering tone, and press Start.
5. Remove portion when done and lay on a cooling rack until cool to slice.

1¼ cup in addition to 1 tablespoon water 2 tablespoons vegetable oil

3 cups bread flour

¾ cup broke wheat

1½ teaspoons salt

2 tablespoons sugar

2¼ teaspoons dynamic dry yeast

1. Bring water to a boil.
2. Place broke wheat in little blending bowl, pour water over it and stir.
3. Cool to 80°F (27°C).
4. Place broke wheat combination into container, trailed by all fixings (with the exception of yeast) in the request listed.
5. Make a well in the focal point of the dry fixings and add the yeast.
6. Select the Basic cycle, medium shading hull, and press Start.
7. Check mixture consistency following 5 minutes of plying. The batter ought to be a delicate, tasteless ball. Assuming that it is dry and firm, add water each ½ tablespoon in turn until tacky. Assuming that it's excessively wet and tacky, add 1 tablespoon of flour at a time.
8. Remove bread when cycle is done and permit to cool before serving.

2 tablespoons full adjusted

yeast 2 cups white bread flour

1½ tablespoons

sugar 1 tablespoon

salt

1 cup water

For the Topping:

Olive oil

Poppy

seeds

1. Add water first, then, at that point, add the dry fixings to the bread machine, holding yeast.
2. Make a well in the focal point of the dry fixings and add the yeast.

3. Choose French cycle, light hull tone, and push Start.
4. When bread is done, cover the highest point of portion with a little olive oil and daintily sprinkle with poppy seeds.
5. Allow to cool marginally and serve warm with additional olive oil for dipping.

½ cup warm water
½ cup warm milk
1 egg
⅓ cup spread, unsalted and softened
⅓ cup sugar
1 teaspoon salt
3¾ cups generally useful flour
1 (¼-ounce/7.1-g) bundle dynamic dry yeast
¼ cup margarine, relaxed
Flour, for surface

1. Place fixings in the bread container in the accompanying request: water, milk, egg, spread, sugar, salt, and flour. Save yeast.
2. Make a well in the focal point of the dry fixings and add the yeast.
3. Select Dough cycle and press Start.
4. When cycle gets done, turn mixture out onto a gently floured surface.
5. Divide batter down the middle and roll every half into a 12-inch circle, spread ¼ cup mellowed margarine over whole round. Cut each circle into 8 wedges. Roll wedges beginning at the wide end and roll delicately however tight.
6. Place point side down on ungreased treat sheet. Cover with clean kitchen towel and put in a warm spot, let rise 1 hour.
7. Preheat broiler to 400°F (205°C) and heat rolls in preheated stove for 10 to 15 minutes, until golden.
8. Serve warm.

2 new eggs, at room temperature

1 cup milk

¼ cup margarine, unsalted, at room temperature

¾ cup sugar

1 teaspoon salt

2 cups unbleached generally useful

flour 1 cup cornmeal

1 tablespoon baking powder

1. Add every one of the fixings to your bread machine in the request listed.
2. Select the Quick Bread cycle, light hull tone, and press Start.
3. Allow to cool for five minutes on a wire rack and serve warm.

1 cup, in addition to 2

tablespoons water 3

tablespoons agave nectar

2 tablespoons spread,

unsalted 1½ cups bread

flour

1½ cups entire wheat flour

¼ cup fragmented almonds,

toasted 1 teaspoon salt

1½ teaspoons speedy dynamic dry yeast

1. Add each of the fixings in bread machine container as per the pattern in which they show up above, saving yeast.
2. Make a well in the focal point of the dry fixings and add the yeast.
3. Select the Basic cycle, light or medium outside shading, and press Start.
4. Remove prepared bread from skillet and cool on a rack before slicing.

1 cup warm

water 1 egg
white, beaten 2
tablespoons oil
3 cups universally handy flour
½ teaspoon salt
1 tablespoon granulated
sugar 1 bundle dry yeast
Coarse ocean salt, for topping
⅓ cup baking pop (for bubbling
interaction) Flour, for surface

1. Place the fixings in bread machine dish in the request recorded above, saving yeast
2. Make a well in the focal point of the dry fixings and add the yeast.
3. Select Dough cycle and press Start.
4. Remove the mixture out onto a softly floured surface and separation batter into four parts.
5. Roll the four sections into balls.
6. Place on lubed treat sheet and let rise uncovered for around 20 minutes or until puffy.
7. In a 3-quart pot, consolidate 2 quarts of water and baking pop and bring to a boil.
8. Preheat a broiler to 425°F (220°C).
9. Lower 2 pretzels into the pan and stew for 10 seconds on each side.
10. Lift from water with an opened spoon and return to lubed treat sheet; rehash with remaining pretzels.
11. Let dry briefly.
12. Brush with egg white and sprinkle with coarse salt.
13. Bake in preheated stove for 20 minutes or until brilliant brown.
14. Let cool somewhat before serving.

Italian Breadsticks
Serves 12 to 16

1½ cups warm water

2 tablespoons margarine, unsalted and liquefied 4¼ cups bread flour

2 tablespoons sugar

1 tablespoon salt

1 bundle dynamic dry yeast

For the Topping:

1 stick unsalted spread, dissolved 2 teaspoons garlic powder

1 teaspoons salt

1 teaspoon parsley

1. Add wet fixings to your bread machine pan.
2. Mix dry fixings, with the exception of yeast, and add to pan.
3. Make a well in the focal point of the dry fixings and add the yeast.
4. Set to Dough cycle and press Start.
5. When the batter is done, carry out and cut into strips; remember that they will twofold in size after they have risen, so carry them out more slender than a normal breadstick to yield space for them to grow.
6. Place on a lubed baking sheet.
7. Cover the mixture with a light towel and let sit in a warm region for 45 minutes to an hour.
8. Preheat a stove to 400°F (205°C).
9. Bake breadsticks for 6 to 7 minutes.
10. Mix the softened margarine, garlic powder, salt and parsley in a little blending bowl.
11. Brush the bread sticks with a large portion of the spread combination; return to broiler and prepare for 5 to 8 extra minutes.
12. Remove breadsticks from the stove and brush the other portion of the margarine mixture.
13. Allow to cool for a couple of moments before serving.

Corn Bagels

Serves 9

1 cup warm water
1½ teaspoons salt
2 tablespoons sugar
3 cups bread flour
2¼ teaspoons dynamic dry yeast
3 quarts bubbling water
3 tablespoons white sugar
1 tablespoon cornmeal
1 egg white
Flour, for surface

1. Place in the bread machine container in the accompanying request: warm water, salt, sugar, and flour.
2. Make a well in the focal point of the dry fixings and add the yeast.
3. Select Dough cycle and press Start.
4. When Dough cycle is finished, eliminate dish and let mixture lay on a gently floured surface. Mix 3 tablespoons of sugar into the bubbling water.
5. Cut mixture into 9 equivalent pieces and roll each piece into a little ball.
6. Flatten each ball with the center of your hand. Punch a hole in each utilizing your thumb. Whirl the batter on your finger to make the opening greater, while evening out the mixture around the hole.
7. Sprinkle an ungreased baking sheet with 1 teaspoon cornmeal. Place the bagel on the baking sheet and rehash until all bagels are formed.
8. Cover the molded bagels with a perfect kitchen towel and let ascend for 10 minutes.

9. Preheat a stove to 375°F (190°C).
10. Carefully move the bagels, individually, to the bubbling water. Bubble for 1 moment, turning halfway.
11. Drain on a perfect towel. Orchestrate bubbled bagels on the baking sheet.
12. Glaze the tops with egg white and sprinkle any fixings you desire.
13. Bake for 20 to 25 minutes or until brilliant brown.
14. Let cool on a wire rack before serving.

1 cup Amish Friendship Bread
Starter 3 eggs
⅔ cup vegetable oil
¼ cup
milk 1
cup sugar
½ teaspoon vanilla
concentrate 2 teaspoons
cinnamon
1½ teaspoons baking powder
½ teaspoon salt
½ teaspoon baking
soft drink 2 cups
flour
2 little boxes moment vanilla pudding

1. Add each of the wet fixings into the bread machine pan.
2. Add in dry fixings, with the exception of sugar and cinnamon.
3. Set bread machine on Sweet cycle, light hull tone and press Start.
4. During the most recent 30 minutes of baking, lift cover and as soon as possible add ¼ cup sugar and ¼ teaspoon of cinnamon.
5. When completed the process of baking, leave in bread machine for 20 minutes to rest.
6. Remove from baking dish and put portion on a cooling rack.

1¼ cups milk
1 egg
2 tablespoons butter
¾ teaspoon salt
¼ cup white sugar
3¾ cups universally handy flour
1 bundle dynamic dry yeast
Flour, for surface

1. Add all fixings to the skillet of your bread machine in the request recorded above.
2. Set bread machine to Dough cycle. When the Dough cycle is finished, carry batter out on a floured surface to around a 1-inch thickness.
3. Cut out 18 buns with a bread roll shaper or little glass and spot them on a lubed baking sheet.
4. Let buns ascend around one hour or until they have multiplied in size.
5. Bake at 350°F (180°C) for 10 minutes.
6. Brush the highest points of heated buns with liquefied spread and serve.

¼ cup milk
2 eggs
4 tablespoons butter
1½ tablespoons vanilla sugar
¼ teaspoon salt
2 cups flour
1½ teaspoon yeast
1 egg white, for finishing

1. Place wet fixings (aside from egg white for getting done) into your bread machine.
2. Add dry fixings, aside from yeast.
3. Make a well inside the flour and afterward add the yeast into the well.
4. Set to Dough cycle and press Start.
5. Remove mixture, place batter on floured surface and separation into 12 equivalent size rolls.
6. Pinch pecan estimated chunk of batter off each roll, making a more modest ball; make indent on top of roll and wet with milk; connect little ball to top making the customary brioche shape.
7. Let ascend for 30 minutes until practically twofold in size.
8. Preheat broiler to 375°F (190°C).
9. Beat egg white, brush highest points of brioche rolls, and prepare at 375°F (190°C) for 10 to 12 minutes, or until brilliant on top. Cool on rack before serving.

1¼ cups milk, marginally warmed 1 egg, beaten
2 tablespoons spread, unsalted
¼ cup white sugar
¾ teaspoon salt
3¾ cups bread flour
1¼ teaspoons dynamic dry yeast Flour, for surface

1. Place all fixings into the container of the bread machine in the accompanying request, saving yeast: milk, egg, margarine, sugar, salt, flour.
2. Make a well in the focal point of the dry fixings and add the yeast.
3. Select Dough cycle. At the point when cycle is finished, turn out onto floured surface.
4. Cut mixture fifty-fifty and carry every half out to a 1" thick circle.
5. Cut every half into 6 (3½") adjusts with upset glass as a shaper. (For wiener buns, cut longwise into 1-inch-thick rolls, and cut a cut

along the length of the bun for more straightforward partition later.)
6. Place on a lubed baking sheet far separated and brush with dissolved butter.
7. Cover and let ascend until multiplied, around 60 minutes; preheat a broiler to 350°F (180°C).
8. Bake for 9 minutes.
9. Let cool and present with your beloved meats and toppings!

Chapter 3: Breakfast Breads

Breakfast Cinnamon Swirl
Makes 2 pounds

For the Dough:
1⅓ cups water
3 tablespoons unsalted spread, cut into pieces
⅓ cup sugar
4 cups bread flour
¼ cup dry buttermilk powder
1 tablespoon in addition to 1
teaspoon gluten 1½ teaspoons
salt
2½ teaspoons SAF yeast or 1 tablespoon bread machine yeast

For the Cinnamon Swirl:
2 tablespoons unsalted margarine, liquefied, for brushing
⅓ cup light brown sugar
1 tablespoon ground cinnamon

1. Place every one of the fixings in the dish as indicated by the request in the maker's directions. Set covering on medium and set to Basic cycle.
2. After Rise 2 finishes on the Basic cycle, press Pause, eliminate the dish, and close the top. Quickly turn the batter out onto a softly floured work surface; pat into a 8-by-12-inch fat square shape.

Brush with the dissolved spread. Sprinkle with the sugar and cinnamon, leaving a 1-inch space as far as possible around the edge. Beginning at a short edge, roll the mixture up jam roll style. Fold the finishes under and squeeze the base crease. Cover the lower part of the batter with cooking shower, eliminate the manipulating cutting edge, and spot the mixture back in the skillet; press Start to proceed to rise and heat as customized. At the point when the baking cycle closes, promptly eliminate the bread from the pan.

3. When the machine signals toward the finish of the cycle, eliminate the container and turn the batter out onto a softly floured work surface. Pat the 2 pounds (907 g) mixture into two 8-by-12-inch square shapes. Brush the rectangle(s) with liquefied margarine. Sprinkle with the earthy colored sugar and

cinnamon, leaving a 1-inch edge as far as possible around. Beginning at a short end, roll up jam roll design. Fold the closures under and squeeze the base seam.

4. Place the single enormous portion in the pre-arranged 9-by-5-inch skillet or the two more modest portions in the 7-by-4-inch container. Splash the top(s) with cooking shower and cover daintily with saran wrap. Let ascend at room temperature until multiplied in mass, around 45 minutes. Heat for 35 to
40 minutes, or until brilliant brown and the sides have marginally contracted from the dish. Assuming the outside layer browns excessively fast, place a piece of aluminum foil freely over the top.

5. Place the bread on a rack and let cool to room temperature prior to cutting. Dust with plain or vanilla confectioners' sugar, if desired.

¾ cup sugar cubes

2 teaspoons ground cinnamon Small touch of ground cloves 1⅓ cups without fat milk

2 tablespoons unsalted spread or margarine, cut into pieces 4 cups bread flour

1 tablespoon in addition to 1 teaspoon gluten 1¾ teaspoons salt

2½ teaspoons SAF yeast or 1 tablespoon bread machine yeast

1. Place the sugar solid shapes in a weighty clear plastic cooler sack and, utilizing the smooth side of a meat hammer, break the blocks. Try not to squash them; you need the pieces to be no more modest than quarter solid shapes, if conceivable. Add the flavors to the pack and throw to cover. Set aside.
2. Place the fixings, with the exception of the zest covered sugar 3D shapes, in the container as per the request in the producer's directions. Set covering on medium, and program for the Sweet Bread cycle; press Start. 5 minutes into the working section, press Pause and sprinkle in portion of the sugar 3D square blend. Press Start to continue the cycle. after 3 minutes, press Pause and add the remainder of the sugar 3D square blend. Press Start to continue the cycle.
3. When the baking cycle closes, promptly eliminate the bread from the dish and spot it on a rack. Let cool to room temperature prior to cutting, or sugar syrup will overflow out.

1⅓ cups dull

raisins 1½ cups

buttermilk 1 huge

egg

2½ tablespoons canola oil

3 tablespoons dim earthy

colored sugar 4 cups bread

flour

1 tablespoon in addition to 2 teaspoons gluten

2 teaspoons salt

2¼ teaspoons SAF yeast or 2¾ teaspoons bread machine yeast

1. Place the raisins in a little bowl to warm in the microwave or in a little dish to warm on the oven. Cover with water and hotness to bubbling. Let represent 10 minutes to full, then, at that point, channel on paper towels.
2. Place the fixings, with the exception of the raisins, in the skillet as indicated by the request in the producer's guidelines. Set outside

layer on medium and program for the Sweet Bread or Fruit and Nut cycle; press Start. At the point when the machine signals, or between Knead 1 and Knead 2, add the raisins.

3. When the baking cycle closes, quickly eliminate the bread from the dish and spot it on a rack. Let cool to room temperature before slicing.

1⅓ cups buttermilk

2 huge egg whites, daintily beaten

¼ cup canola

oil 2 cups bread

flour

2 cups entire wheat flour

⅓ cup rolled oats

⅓ cup dim earthy

colored sugar 2½

tablespoons gluten

2 teaspoons salt

1½ teaspoons ground

cinnamon 1½ teaspoons

vanilla powder

1 tablespoon SAF yeast or 1 tablespoon in addition to ½ teaspoon bread machine yeast

⅔ cup currants

⅓ cup slashed walnuts

1. Place the fixings, with the exception of the products of the soil, in the container as indicated by the request in the maker's guidelines. Set outside on dull and program for the Basic or Fruit and Nut cycle; press Start. At the point when the machine blares, or between Knead 1 and Knead 2, add the products of the soil. Try not to be enticed to add in excess of a tablespoon of additional flour. This is a clammy mixture ball that will at first look extremely tacky, particularly around the sharp edge. It will change to cheap before the finish of the working and be smooth and sparkling with the rises.

2. When the baking cycle closes, quickly eliminate the bread from the skillet and spot it on a rack. Let cool to room temperature before slicing.

1⅓ cups currants

¼ cup orange juice

One 2-inch piece cinnamon stick 2 entire cloves

Pinch of ground mastika or allspice

1⅛ cups in addition to 1 tablespoon vanished milk 2 teaspoons orange-bloom water

¼ cup honey

4 cups bread flour 1 tablespoon plus 1 teaspoon gluten

2 teaspoons salt

2½ teaspoons SAF yeast or 1 tablespoon bread machine yeast

1. Place the currants in a little bowl. Add the squeezed orange, cinnamon stick, cloves, and mastika or allspice. Throw to join. Cover and let remain at room temperature for 60 minutes. The currants will be delicate and full. Eliminate and dispose of the cinnamon stick and cloves.
2. Drain and save any additional squeezed orange from the currants. Add 3 tablespoons water to the juice.
3. Place the fixings, aside from the currants, in the skillet as indicated by the request in the maker's guidelines, adding the juice and water blend with the fluid fixings. Set hull on medium and program for the Sweet Bread or Fruit and Nut cycle; press Start. At the point when the machine signals, or between Knead 1 and Knead 2, add the currants.
4. When the baking cycle closes, quickly eliminate the bread from the dish and spot it on a rack. Let cool to room temperature before slicing.

⅔ cup milk

½ cup water

3 tablespoons unsalted spread, cut into pieces 1 huge egg

3 cups bread flour

1 cup entire wheat baked good flour

¼ cup in addition to 1 tablespoon poppy seeds 3 tablespoons sugar

Grated zing of 1 lemon

1 tablespoon in addition to 1 teaspoon gluten

2 teaspoons salt

2½ teaspoons SAF yeast or 1 tablespoon bread machine yeast

¾ cup hacked pitted prunes

1. Place the fixings, with the exception of the prunes, in the dish as indicated by the request in the maker's directions. Set outside on medium and program for the Basic or Fruit and Nut cycle; press Start. At the point when the machine blares, or between Knead 1 and Knead 2, add the prunes.
2. When the baking cycle closes, quickly eliminate the bread from the container and spot it on a rack. Let cool to room temperature before slicing.

1⅔ cups water

2½ tablespoons unsalted margarine, liquefied 3 tablespoons light brown sugar

4 cups bread flour

⅓ cup nonfat dry milk

1 tablespoon in addition to 2 teaspoons gluten

2 teaspoons salt

1¼ teaspoons ground cardamom

2½ teaspoons SAF yeast or 1 tablespoon bread machine yeast

¾ cup brilliant raisins

¾ cup dried cranberries

1. Place the fixings, with the exception of the natural product, in the skillet as per the request in the maker's directions. Set outside on light and program for the Sweet Bread or Fruit and Nut cycle; press Start. At the point when the machine signals, or between Knead 1 and Knead 2, add the fruit.
2. When the baking cycle closes, quickly eliminate the bread from the container and spot it on a rack. Let cool to room temperature before slicing.

1⅓ cups milk

3 tablespoons unsalted margarine, cut into

pieces 1 (8-ounce/227-g) banana, sliced

2½ cups bread flour

1½ cups entire wheat cake flour

¾ cup rolled oats

3 tablespoons sugar

1 tablespoon in addition to 1

teaspoon gluten 1¼ teaspoons salt

1 tablespoon SAF yeast or 1 tablespoon in addition to ½ teaspoon bread machine yeast

½ cup slashed salted macadamia nuts

1. Place the fixings, aside from the nuts, in the dish as indicated by the request in the maker's directions. Set outside on medium and program for the Sweet Bread or Fruit and Nut cycle; press Start. At the point when the machine blares, or between Knead 1 and Knead 2, add the macadamia nuts.
2. When the baking cycle closes, promptly eliminate the bread from the container and spot it on a rack. Let cool to room temperature before slicing.

1¾ cups mandarin orange portions, fluid reserved

3 tablespoons held orange fluid or orange alcohol 4

tablespoons unsalted margarine, cut into pieces

4 cups bread flour

⅓ cup sugar

1 tablespoon gluten

2 teaspoons salt

2¼ teaspoons SAF yeast or 2¾ teaspoons bread machine yeast

⅔ cup white chocolate chips

½ cup minced dried apricots

½ cup slashed walnuts

1. Place the fixings, aside from the white chocolate chips, apricots, and pecans, in the skillet as indicated by the request in the maker's guidelines. Set hull on medium and program for the Basic or Sweet Bread cycle; press Start. The batter ball will ini-tially look dry; don't be enticed to add more fluid. At the point when the machine blares, or between Knead 1 and Knead 2, add the chips, apricots, and walnuts.
2. When the baking cycle closes, quickly eliminate the bread from the dish and spot it on a rack. Let cool to room temperature before slicing.

1½ cups buttermilk

2½ tablespoons pecan

oil 4 cups bread flour

¼ cup light brown sugar

1 tablespoon in addition to 1

teaspoon gluten 1½ teaspoons salt

1⅓ tablespoons ground cinnamon

2½ teaspoons SAF yeast or 1 tablespoon bread machine yeast

⅔ cup slashed dried apples

½ cup hacked pecans

1. Place the fixings, with the exception of the apples and walnuts, in the dish as per the request in the maker's guidelines. Set hull on medium and program for the Basic or Fruit and Nut cycle; press Start. At the point when the machine blares, or between Knead 1

2. When the baking cycle closes, promptly eliminate the bread from the skillet and spot it on a rack. Let cool to room temperature before slicing.

1 cup dried cranberries
3 tablespoons brandy
1 cup water
½ cup pumpkin purée
3 tablespoons nut oil
4 cups bread flour
¼ cup light brown sugar
3 tablespoons dry buttermilk powder
1 tablespoon in addition to 1 teaspoon gluten
2 teaspoons salt
1¾ teaspoons pumpkin or fruity dessert spice
2½ teaspoons SAF yeast or 1 tablespoon bread machine yeast

1. Sprinkle the dried cranberries with the cognac in a little bowl. Cover with cling wrap and let remain at room temperature for 1 hour to macerate.
2. Place the fixings, aside from the cranberries, in the skillet as per the request in the producer's guidelines. Set covering on medium and program for the Sweet Bread cycle; press Start. At the point when the machine blares, or between Knead 1 and Knead 2, add the cranberries and any additional liquor in the bowl.
3. When the baking cycle closes, quickly eliminate the bread from the dish and spot it on a rack. Let cool to room temperature before slicing.

For the Dough:
⅔ cup orange juice

½ cup milk
1 enormous egg
4 tablespoons unsalted margarine, cut into pieces
4 cups bread flour
⅓ cup sugar
Grated zing of 1 orange
1 tablespoon in addition to 1 teaspoon gluten
2½ teaspoons ground cinnamon
1½ teaspoons salt
2¼ teaspoons SAF yeast or 2¾ teaspoons bread machine yeast

For the Vanilla-Orange Glaze:
¾ cup filtered confectioners' sugar
1½ to 2 tablespoons squeezed orange
1 teaspoon vanilla extract

1. To make the batter, place all the mixture fixings in the skillet as per the request in the maker's guidelines. Set hull on medium and program for the Basic cycle; press Start.
2. When the baking cycle closes, promptly eliminate the bread from the container and spot it on a rack. Place a plate or piece of waxed paper under the rack.
3. To set up the coating, join the confectioners' sugar, squeezed orange, and vanilla in a little bowl; beat with a little race until smooth. With a huge spoon, shower the bread with the coating, allowing it to dribble down the sides. Cool to room temperature to set the coating before slicing.

2 huge Hachiya persimmons
1 cup milk
1 enormous egg

1½ tablespoons golden rum
3 tablespoons margarine, cut into pieces
4 cups bread flour
3 tablespoons dim earthy colored sugar
1 tablespoon gluten
2 teaspoons fruity dessert zest
2 teaspoons salt
2½ teaspoons SAF yeast or 1 tablespoon bread machine yeast
1 cup brilliant raisins

1. Cut the delicate persimmons fifty-fifty and scoop out the inward tissue with a huge spoon. Measure out and hold ¾ cup for the portion.
2. Place the fixings, aside from the raisins, in the dish as per the request in the producer's directions, adding the saved persimmon mash with the fluid fixings. Set hull on dull and program for the Basic or Fruit and Nut cycle; press Start. At the point when the machine signals, or between Knead 1 and Knead 2, add the raisins. The mixture ball will be delicate and springy.
3. When the baking cycle closes, promptly eliminate the bread from the skillet and spot it on a rack. Let cool to room temperature prior to cutting. The bread is extremely delicate, so be certain not to cut it before it cools.

½ cup milk
¾ cup ricotta cheddar
3 enormous egg yolks
2 teaspoons anise extract
½ cup (1 stick) in addition to 1 tablespoon unsalted spread, cut into pieces
4 cups bread flour
½ cup walnuts

½ cup brilliant raisins
3½ tablespoons sugar
Grated zing of 2
lemons
1 tablespoon in addition to 1 teaspoon gluten
2 teaspoons salt
2½ teaspoons SAF yeast or 1 tablespoon bread machine yeast

1. Place every one of the fixings in the container as per the request in the maker's guidelines. Set outside on medium and program for the Basic cycle; press Start.
2. When the baking cycle closes, quickly eliminate the bread from the dish and spot it on a rack. Let cool to room temperature before slicing.

1⅔ cups milk
¾ teaspoon almond extract
1½ tablespoons margarine, cut into pieces
4 tablespoons almond glue, cut into
pieces 4 cups bread flour
¼ cup sugar
1 tablespoon in addition to 1 teaspoon gluten
2 teaspoons salt
2½ teaspoons SAF yeast or 1 tablespoon bread machine yeast
⅔ cup hacked dried sharp cherries
⅓ cup fragmented whitened almonds

1. Place the fixings, aside from the cherries and almonds, in the skillet as per the request in the producer's directions. Set hull on medium and program for the Basic or Fruit and Nut cycle; press Start. At the point when the machine blares, or between Knead 1 and Knead 2, add the cherries and almonds.
2. When the baking cycle closes, promptly eliminate the bread from the dish and spot it on a rack. Let cool to room temperature before slicing.

For the Dough:
¼ cup in addition to 1 tablespoon milk
¼ cup water
1 huge egg
3 tablespoons unsalted spread, somewhat liquefied
2½ cups unbleached universally handy flour
¼ cup sugar
1 teaspoon salt
2 teaspoons SAF yeast or 2½ teaspoons bread machine yeast

For the Fruit Filling:
¾ cup dry red wine
¼ cup kirsch
¼ cup sugar
Grated zing of 1 lemon
½ teaspoon ground cinnamon
¼ teaspoon new ground nutmeg
8 ounces (227 g) dried pears, chopped
6 ounces (170 g) dried figs, stemmed and hacked
4 ounces (113 g) pitted prunes
¼ cup raisins
1 egg yolk beaten with 1 tablespoon milk, for glaze

1. To make the mixture, place all the batter fixings in the dish as per the request in the producer's directions. Program for the Dough cycle; press Start. The batter ball will be firm, yet pliable.
2. While the mixture is rising, make the filling. Consolidate the wine, kirsch, sugar, zing, and flavors in a little pan and bring to a boil.

Lower hotness and add the dried organic product. Stew, revealed, for 10 minutes. Eliminate from the hotness, cover, and let remain until room temperature and all of the fluid is retained, around 60 minutes. Place in a food processor and heartbeat to make a thick jam that isn't absolutely smooth.

3. Line a baking sheet with material paper. To gather the portion, when the machine signals toward the finish of the cycle, press Stop and turn off the machine. Turn the batter out onto a delicately floured work surface. With a moving pin, carry out into a 12-by-16-inch square shape. With a metal spatula, spread the filling uniformly over the mixture, leaving ½-inch verges on three sides and a 1-inch verge on one long side. Starting at the long edge with the ½-inch line, roll up jam roll design to make a log. Saturate the 1-inch line with some water and seal. Squeeze the base crease, leaving the closures open. Press to even the closures. Utilizing the prongs of a fork, prick the mixture everywhere. Brush with the egg coat. Let rest at room temperature, covered freely with a perfect tea towel, until multiplied in mass, around 45 minutes.
4. Twenty minutes prior to baking, preheat the stove to 350°F (180°C).
5. Brush the roll again with the egg coat. Heat for 30 to 40 minutes, until brilliant brown and firm to the touch. Let cool on the baking sheet.

1 cup apple or pear
juice 7 tablespoons
water
2½ tablespoons honey
2½ tablespoons nut or vegetable
oil 2⅓ cups bread flour
1 cup entire wheat flour
⅔ cup rolled oats
1 tablespoon in addition to 1
teaspoon gluten 1½ teaspoons salt
2½ teaspoons SAF yeast or 1 tablespoon bread machine yeast
⅔ cup finely hacked dried apricots

1. Place the fixings, with the exception of the apricots, in the dish as indicated by the request in the maker's directions. Set outside on medium and program for the Whole Wheat or Fruit and Nut cycle; press Start. At the point when the machine blares, or between Knead 1 and Knead 2, add the apricots. The batter ball will be delicate and moist.
2. When the baking cycle closes, quickly eliminate the bread from the

container and spot it on a rack. Let cool to room temperature before slicing.

1½ cups buttermilk

3 tablespoons vegetable oil

3 tablespoons honey

2¾ cups bread flour

1 cup entire wheat flour

1⅓ cups granola

1 tablespoon in addition to 1 teaspoon gluten

2 teaspoons salt

1½ teaspoons ground cinnamon

2½ teaspoons SAF yeast or 1 tablespoon bread machine yeast

1. Place every one of the fixings in the dish as per the request in the maker's guidelines. Set outside on medium and program for the Basic cycle; press Start.
2. When the baking cycle closes, quickly eliminate the bread from the skillet and spot it on a rack. Let cool to room temperature before slicing.

Chapter 4: Whole-Wheat Breads
Basic Whole Wheat Bread
Makes 1 pound

½ cup tepid entire milk

2 tablespoons unsalted spread, diced

1 cup entire wheat flour

1 cup torment bread flour

2½ tablespoons brown sugar

¾ teaspoon salt

¾ teaspoon bread machine yeast

1. Add the fixings into the bread machine according to the request for the fixings recorded above or adhere to your bread machine's

guidance manual.
2. Select the Whole Wheat cycle and medium outside layer function.
3. When prepared, turn the bread out onto a drying rack and permit it to cool, then, at that point, serve.

1⅛ cups tepid water 3
tablespoons honey
2 tablespoons vegetable
oil 1½ cups plain bread
flour 1½ cups entire
wheat flour
⅓ teaspoon salt
1½ teaspoons moment dry yeast

1. Add the fixings into the bread machine according to the request for the fixings recorded above or adhere to your bread machine's guidance manual.
2. Select the Whole Wheat cycle and medium covering function.
3. When prepared, turn the bread out onto a drying rack and permit it to cool, then, at that point, serve.

⅔ cup tepid water 1
tablespoon olive oil
2 tablespoons maple syrup
1¾ cups white entire wheat flour
6 teaspoons grouped seeds (an even blend of flax, sesame and additionally sunflower seeds)
¾ teaspoon salt
¾ teaspoon moment yeast

1. Place all fixings into your bread machine in the specific request listed.
2. Select the entire wheat setting and the medium hull function.
3. When prepared, turn the bread out onto a drying rack so it can cool, then, at that point, serve.

1 cup tepid water
1¼ tablespoons milk powder
1¼ tablespoons unsalted
margarine, diced 1¼ tablespoons
honey
1¼ tablespoons
molasses 1 teaspoon
salt
2¼ cups entire wheat
flour 1 teaspoon
dynamic dry yeast

1. Add the fixings into the bread machine according to the request for the fixings recorded above or adhere to your bread machine's guidance manual.
2. Select the Whole Wheat cycle and medium outside layer function.
3. When prepared, turn the bread out onto a drying rack and permit it to cool, then, at that point, serve.

3 tablespoons milk
powder 1 tablespoon
honey
1 tablespoon unsalted spread,
relaxed 1 cup plain bread flour
1 cup entire wheat flour
2 tablespoons poppy
seeds 2 tablespoons
sesame seeds
2 tablespoons sunflower seeds
¾ teaspoon salt
2 teaspoons moment dry yeast

1. Add the fixings into the bread machine according to the request for the fixings recorded above or adhere to your bread machine's guidance manual.

2. Select the Basic cycle and medium hull function.
3. When prepared, turn the bread out onto a drying rack and permit it to cool, then, at that point, serve.

½ tablespoon olive oil
8 teaspoons honey
½ cup rolled oats
¾ cup entire wheat flour
¾ cup white bread flour
½ teaspoon salt
½ teaspoon moment yeast

1. All fixings ought to enter your bread machine either in the request recorded or as per your bread machine's guidance manual.
2. Select the Basic cycle and delicate hull function.
3. When prepared, turn the bread out onto a drying rack so it can cool, then, at that point, serve.

1 cup bubbling water
⅔ cup broke wheat or bulgur
¼ cup molasses
3 tablespoons unsalted margarine or margarine, cut into pieces
2 teaspoons salt
1 cup water
3½ cups bread flour
½ cup entire wheat flour
1 tablespoon in addition to 1 teaspoon gluten
1 tablespoon SAF yeast or 1 tablespoon in addition to ½ teaspoon bread machine yeast

1. Pour the bubbling water over the broke wheat in a bowl. Add the molasses, margarine, and salt. Let stand 1 hour at room temperature to soften.
2. Place the fixings in the skillet as per the request in the producer's guidelines, adding the broke wheat combination and the extra

water as the fluid fixings. Set covering on medium and program for the Basic cycle; press Start.

3. When the baking cycle closes, quickly eliminate the bread from the dish and spot it on a rack. Let cool to room temperature before slicing.

1⅓ cups water
1 enormous egg in addition to 1 egg yolk
3 tablespoons margarine, cut into
pieces 3 cups bread flour
1 cup graham flour
½ cup nonfat dry milk
⅓ cup light earthy
colored sugar 1
tablespoon gluten
2 teaspoons salt
2¼ teaspoons SAF yeast or 2¾ teaspoons bread machine yeast

1. Place every one of the fixings in the skillet as indicated by the request in the producer's directions. Set outside on medium and program for the Basic or Whole Wheat cycle; press Start.
2. When the baking cycle closes, quickly eliminate the bread from the container and spot it on a rack. Let cool to room temperature before slicing.

1⅔ cups water
4 tablespoons margarine, cut into
pieces 3 tablespoons honey
2½ cups entire wheat
flour 1½ cups bread
flour
⅓ cup moment potato
drops 2 tablespoons
gluten
2 teaspoons salt

2½ teaspoons SAF yeast or 1 tablespoon bread machine yeast

1. Place every one of the fixings in the dish as per the request in the maker's directions. Set hull on medium and program for the Whole Wheat cycle; press Start.
2. When the baking cycle closes, promptly eliminate the bread from the dish and spot it on a rack. Let cool to room temperature before slicing.

1½ cups water
3 tablespoons canola oil
¼ cup honey
2⅔ cups bread flour
1⅓ cups entire wheat flour
⅓ cup nonfat dry milk
2½ tablespoons flax
seed 1¼ tablespoons
gluten 1½ teaspoons
salt
2¼ teaspoons SAF yeast or 2¾ teaspoons bread machine yeast

1. Place every one of the fixings in the container as per the request in the producer's guidelines. Set hull on medium and program for the Basic or Whole Wheat cycle; press Start.
2. When the baking cycle closes, promptly eliminate the bread from the skillet and spot it on a rack. Let cool to room temperature before slicing.

3 tablespoons
honey 21 cups
bread flour
1 cup entire wheat flour
⅓ cup crude bulgur broke
wheat 1 tablespoon gluten
2 teaspoons salt
⅓ cup crude sunflower seeds

⅓ cup crude pumpkin seeds,
hacked 2 teaspoons sesame seeds
2 teaspoons poppy seeds
2¼ teaspoons SAF yeast or 2¾ teaspoons bread machine yeast

1. Place every one of the fixings in the container as per the request in the maker's directions. Set outside on dim and program for the Basic cycle; press Start.
2. When the baking cycle closes, promptly eliminate the bread from the dish and spot it on a rack. Let cool to room temperature before slicing.

2½ tablespoons maple
syrup 2 cups entire wheat
flour
2 cups bread flour
1 tablespoon in addition to 2 teaspoons gluten
2 teaspoons salt
2¼ teaspoons SAF yeast or 2¾ teaspoons bread machine yeast

1. Place every one of the fixings in the dish as per the request in the maker's directions. Set covering on medium and program for the Basic or Whole Wheat cycle; press Start.
2. When the baking cycle closes, promptly eliminate the bread from the skillet and spot it on a rack. Let cool to room temperature before slicing.

¼ cup
honey 2
huge eggs
4 tablespoons spread or margarine, cut into
pieces 3 cups unbleached universally handy
flour
1 cup entire wheat flour
½ cup toasted raw grain
1½ teaspoons salt

2 teaspoons SAF yeast or 2½ teaspoons bread machine yeast

1. Place every one of the fixings in the container as per the request in the maker's directions. Program for the Dough cycle; press Start.
2. Grease an enormous baking sheet or line with material paper. At the point when the machine blares toward the finish of the cycle, press Stop and turn off the machine. Turn the mixture out onto a daintily floured surface. Divide the dough in half, then roll each half into a 2- to 3-inch cylinder. With a metal mixture scrubber or a gourmet expert's blade, cut the chamber into 8 equivalent segments. Rehash with the subsequent chamber, making a sum of 16 equivalent parts. Shape each portion like a miniature loaf by patting it into an oval, then rolling up from a short side to make a small compact cylinder about 4 inches long. Place the rolls in two columns of 8 with their long sides contacting. Brush a few liquefied spread on the highest points of the rolls. Cover freely with cling wrap and let ascend at room temperature until multiplied in mass, around 45 minutes.
3. 20 minutes prior to baking, preheat the stove to 375°F (190°C).
4. Place the baking sheet in the focal point of the broiler and prepare for 25 minutes, until brilliant brown. Eliminate the rolls from the dish and let cool on a rack. Serve warm, or cool to room temperature and reheat
before serving.

Zest of 2 oranges, cut into
exceptionally meager strips 1⅔ cups
without fat milk
3 tablespoons olive or pecan
oil 3 tablespoons honey
2¼ cups entire wheat
flour 2 cups bread flour
1 tablespoon in addition to 1
teaspoon gluten 1½ teaspoons salt
2¼ teaspoons SAF yeast or 2¾ teaspoons bread machine yeast

1. In a food processor, hack the orange strip fine, or cleave it fine by

hand.
2. Place every one of the fixings in the container as per the request in the maker's directions. Set hull on medium and program for the Whole Wheat cycle; press Start.
3. When the baking cycle closes, quickly eliminate the bread from the skillet and spot it on a rack. Let cool to room temperature before slicing.

1 cup water

3 huge eggs

¼ cup vegetable oil

2½ tablespoons honey

2 cups entire wheat flour

2 cups bread flour

2 tablespoons gluten

1¼ tablespoons moment potato pieces

2 teaspoons salt

2½ teaspoons SAF yeast or 1 tablespoon bread machine yeast

1. Place every one of the fixings in the dish as per the request in the maker's guidelines. Set outside on medium or dim, and program for the Basic or Whole Wheat cycle; press Start. This is a wet mixture ball. Try not to add more flour during the manipulating or the bread will be dry.
2. When Rise 2 closures, press Pause, open the top and lift the warm batter from the skillet. Partition the mixture into 2 equivalent bits. With the centers of your hands, fold each part into a fat elongated frankfurter, about 10 inches long. Place the two pieces one next to the other. Holding each end, fold one over the other, contorting every one simultaneously, to make a fat turn impact. Fold under the finishes and supplant in the container in the machine. The bend shape will prepare in the machine.
3. When the baking cycle closes, promptly eliminate the bread from the container and spot it on a rack. Let cool to room temperature

before slicing.

Chapter 5: Cheese Breads
Chipotle Cheese Bread
Makes 1 pound

⅔ cup water, at 80°F (27°C) to 90°F (32°C) 1½ tablespoons sugar
1½ tablespoons powdered skim milk
¾ teaspoon salt
½ teaspoon chipotle bean stew powder 2 cups white bread flour
½ cup destroyed sharp Cheddar cheese
¾ teaspoon bread machine or moment yeast

1. Place the fixings in your bread machine as suggested by the manufacturer.
2. Set the machine to Basic cycle, select light or medium hull, and press Start.
3. When the portion is done, eliminate the can from the machine.
4. Let the portion cool for 5 minutes.
5. Gently shake the container to eliminate the portion, and turn it out onto a rack to cool.

½ cup in addition to 1 tablespoon milk, at 70°F (21°C) to 80°F (27°C) 2⅔ tablespoons dissolved margarine, cooled
⅔ teaspoon minced garlic 4 teaspoons sugar
⅔ teaspoon salt
⅓ cup ground Asiago cheese
1¾ cups in addition to 1 tablespoon white bread flour 1 teaspoon bread machine or moment yeast

⅓ cup crushed cooked garlic

1. Place the fixings, with the exception of the broiled garlic, in your bread machine as suggested by the manufacturer.
2. Set the machine to Basic cycle, select light or medium outside layer, and press Start.
3. Add the simmered garlic when your machine signs or 5 minutes before the last massaging is done.
4. When the portion is done, eliminate the pail from the machine.
5. Let the portion cool for 5 minutes.
6. Gently shake the can to eliminate the portion, and turn it out onto a rack to cool.

⅔ cup milk, at 80°F (27°C) to 90°F (32°C) 2 teaspoons liquefied spread, cooled
2 teaspoons sugar
⅔ teaspoon dried basil
½ cup destroyed sharp Cheddar cheese
½ teaspoon salt
2 cups white bread flour
1 teaspoon bread machine or dynamic dry yeast

1. Place the fixings in your bread machine as suggested by the manufacturer.
2. Set the machine to Basic cycle, select light or medium covering, and press Start.
3. When the portion is done, eliminate the can from the machine.
4. Let the portion cool for 5 minutes.
5. Gently shake the can to eliminate the portion, and turn it out onto a rack to cool.

1 cup buttermilk, at 80°F (27°C) to 90°F (32°C)
¼ cup softened
margarine, cooled 2 eggs,

at room temperature 1
jalapeño pepper, slashed
1⅓ cups universally
handy flour 1 cup
cornmeal
½ cup destroyed Cheddar cheese
¼ cup sugar
1 tablespoon baking powder
½ teaspoon salt

1. Place the buttermilk, spread, eggs, and jalapeño pepper in your bread machine.
2. Program the machine for Quick cycle and press Start.
3. While the wet fixings are blending, mix together the flour, cornmeal, cheddar, sugar, baking powder, and salt in a little bowl.
4. After the principal quick blending is done and the machine signals, add the dry ingredients.
5. When the portion is done, eliminate the can from the machine.
6. Let the portion cool for 5 minutes.
7. Gently shake the can to eliminate the portion, and turn it out onto a rack to cool.

⅔ cup milk, at 80°F (27°C) to 90°F
(32°C) 1 tablespoon dissolved spread,
cooled
⅔ teaspoon minced
garlic 1 tablespoon sugar
⅔ teaspoon salt
2 cups white bread flour
½ cup destroyed Swiss cheese
¾ teaspoon bread machine or moment yeast
¼ cup hacked dark olives

1. Place the fixings in your bread machine as suggested by the maker,

throwing the flour with the cheddar first.
2. Set the machine to Basic cycle, select light or medium outside, and press Start.
3. When the portion is done, eliminate the can from the machine.
4. Let the portion cool for 5 minutes.
5. Gently shake the can to eliminate the portion, and turn it out onto a rack to cool.

¾ cup in addition to 1 tablespoon water, at 80°F (27°C) to
90°F (32°C) 1 egg, at room temperature
2 teaspoons liquefied margarine,
cooled 3 tablespoons powdered
skim milk 2 teaspoons sugar
½ teaspoon salt
⅓ cup disintegrated blue
cheddar 2 teaspoons dried
onion drops 2 cups white
bread flour
3 tablespoons moment pounded potato pieces
¾ teaspoon bread machine or dynamic dry yeast

1. Place the fixings in your bread machine as suggested by the manufacturer.
2. Set the machine to Basic cycle, select light or medium hull, and press Start.
3. When the portion is done, eliminate the container from the machine.
4. Let the portion cool for 5 minutes.
5. Gently shake the can to eliminate the portion, and turn it out onto a rack to cool.

¾ cup in addition to 1 tablespoon milk, at 80°F (27°C) to
90°F (32°C) 2 teaspoons spread, dissolved and cooled
4 teaspoons sugar
⅔ teaspoon salt

⅓ teaspoon newly ground dark pepper
Pinch cayenne pepper
1 cup destroyed matured sharp Cheddar cheese
⅓ cup destroyed or ground Parmesan cheddar
2 cups white bread flour
¾ teaspoon bread machine or moment yeast

1. Place the fixings in your bread machine as suggested by the manufacturer.
2. Set the machine to Basic cycle, select light or medium outside layer, and press Start.
3. When the portion is done, eliminate the can from the machine.
4. Let the portion cool for 5 minutes.
5. Gently shake the pail to eliminate the portion, and turn it out onto a rack to cool.

¾ cup water, at 80°F (27°C) to 90°F (32°C)
⅓ cup destroyed mozzarella cheddar
4 teaspoons sugar
⅔ teaspoon salt
⅔ teaspoon dried basil
Pinch garlic powder
2 cups in addition to 2 tablespoons white bread flour
1 teaspoon bread machine or moment yeast
½ cup finely diced hot German salami

1. Place the fixings, aside from the salami, in your bread machine as suggested by the manufacturer.
2. Set the machine to Basic cycle, select light or medium covering, and press Start.
3. Add the salami when your machine signs or 5 minutes before the second Kneading cycle is finished.
4. When the portion is done, eliminate the can from the machine.

5. Let the portion cool for 5 minutes.
6. Gently shake the can to eliminate the portion, and turn it out onto a rack to cool.

⅓ cup water, at 80°F (27°C) to 90°F (32°C)
½ cup low-fat curds, at room temperature 1 egg,
at room temperature
4 teaspoons margarine, liquefied
and cooled 2 teaspoons sugar
⅔ teaspoon salt
⅛ teaspoon baking
soft drink 2 cups
white bread flour
1⅓ teaspoons bread machine or moment yeast

1. Place the fixings in your bread machine as suggested by the manufacturer.
2. Set the machine to Basic cycle, select light or medium outside layer, and press Start.
3. When the portion is done, eliminate the can from the machine.
4. Let the portion cool for 5 minutes.
5. Gently shake the can to eliminate the portion, and turn it out onto a rack to cool.

⅓ cup milk, at 80°F (27°C) to 90°F
(32°C) 1 teaspoon liquefied spread,
cooled
1 tablespoon honey
1 teaspoon salt
⅓ cup cleaved and depleted green chiles
⅓ cup ground Cheddar cheese
⅓ cup slashed cooked bacon
2 cups white bread flour
1⅓ teaspoons bread machine or moment yeast

1. Place the fixings in your bread machine as suggested by the manufacturer.
2. Set the machine to Basic cycle, select light or medium hull, and press Start.
3. When the portion is done, eliminate the can from the machine.
4. Let the portion cool for 5 minutes.
5. Gently shake the can to eliminate the portion, and turn it out onto a rack to cool.

¾ cup water, at 80°F (27°C) to 90°F
(32°C) 2 tablespoons dissolved
margarine, cooled
2 teaspoons sugar
⅔ teaspoon salt
1⅓ teaspoons hacked new basil
2⅔ tablespoons ground Parmesan
cheddar 2⅓ cups white bread flour
1 teaspoon bread machine or moment yeast

1. Place the fixings in your bread machine as suggested by the manufacturer.
2. Set the machine to Basic cycle, select light or medium outside layer, and press Start.
3. When the portion is done, eliminate the can from the machine.
4. Let the portion cool for 5 minutes.
5. Gently shake the can to eliminate the portion, and turn it out onto a rack to cool.

4 teaspoons margarine, dissolved
and cooled 2 tablespoons sugar
⅔ teaspoon salt
⅓ cup ground matured cheddar 2
cups white bread flour
1⅓ teaspoons bread machine or moment yeast

1. Place the fixings in your bread machine as suggested by the manufacturer.
2. Set the machine to Basic cycle, select light or medium outside, and press Start.
3. When the portion is done, eliminate the can from the machine.
4. Let the portion cool for 5 minutes.
5. Gently shake the can to eliminate the portion, and turn it out onto a rack to cool.

2 teaspoons softened
margarine, cooled 2 teaspoons
sugar
⅔ teaspoon salt
2 teaspoons dried
oregano 2 cups white
bread flour
1½ teaspoons bread machine or moment yeast
⅔ cup disintegrated feta cheese

1. Place the fixings in your bread machine as suggested by the manufacturer.
2. Set the machine to Basic cycle, select light or medium covering, and press Start.
3. When the portion is done, eliminate the can from the machine.
4. Let the portion cool for 5 minutes.
5. Gently shake the can to eliminate the portion, and turn it out onto a rack to cool.

2⅔ tablespoons goat cheddar, at room
temperature 1 tablespoon honey
⅔ teaspoon salt
⅔ teaspoon newly separated dark
pepper 2 cups white bread flour
1 teaspoon bread machine or moment yeast

1. Place the fixings in your bread machine as suggested by the

manufacturer.
2. Set the machine to Basic cycle, select light or medium outside, and press Start.
3. When the portion is done, eliminate the can from the machine.
4. Let the portion cool for 5 minutes.
5. Gently shake the can to eliminate the portion, and turn it out onto a rack to cool.

¾ cup in addition to 1 tablespoon milk, at 80°F (27°C) to 90°F (32°C) 2 teaspoons spread, softened and cooled

4 teaspoons sugar

⅔ teaspoon salt

1⅓ teaspoons dried basil

⅔ teaspoon dried oregano

1 cup destroyed mozzarella cheddar 2 cups white bread flour

1½ teaspoons bread machine or moment yeast

1. Place the fixings in your bread machine as suggested by the manufacturer.
2. Set the machine to Basic cycle, select light or medium hull, and press Start.
3. When the portion is done, eliminate the can from the machine.
4. Let the portion cool for 5 minutes.
5. Gently shake the can to eliminate the portion, and turn it out onto a rack to cool.

Chapter 6: Fruit Breads

Orange Bread

Makes 1 pound

1¼ cups milk, at 80°F (27°C) to 90°F (32°C)

2 tablespoons newly crushed squeezed orange, at room

temperature 2 tablespoons sugar

¾ tablespoon liquefied margarine, cooled

¾ teaspoon salt

2 cups white bread

flour Zest of ½ orange

1 teaspoon bread machine or moment yeast

1. Place the fixings in your bread machine as suggested by the manufacturer.
2. Set the machine to Basic cycle, select light or medium covering, and press Start.
3. When the portion is done, eliminate the can from the machine.
4. Let the portion cool for 5 minutes.
5. Gently shake the can to eliminate the portion, and turn it out onto a rack to cool.

½ cup milk, at 80°F (27°C) to 90°F (32°C)

2¾ tablespoons unsweetened fruit purée, at room

temperature 2 teaspoons dissolved spread, cooled

2 teaspoons sugar

⅔ teaspoon salt

¼ teaspoon ground

cinnamon Pinch ground

nutmeg

2¾ tablespoons speedy

oats 1½ cups white

bread flour

1½ teaspoons bread machine or dynamic dry yeast

1. Place the fixings in your bread machine as suggested by the manufacturer.
2. Set the machine to Basic cycle, select light or medium covering, and press Start.
3. When the portion is done, eliminate the can from the machine.

4. Let the portion cool for 5 minutes.
5. Gently shake the can to eliminate the portion, and turn it out onto a rack to cool.

¾ cup milk, at 80°F (27°C) to 90°F
(32°C) 2 tablespoons softened spread,
cooled
2 tablespoons sugar
1 teaspoon salt
½ cup cut new strawberries
¾ cup fast oats
1½ cups white bread flour
1 teaspoon bread machine or moment yeast

1. Place the fixings in your bread machine as suggested by the manufacturer.
2. Set the machine to Basic cycle, select light or medium outside, and press Start.
3. When the portion is done, eliminate the can from the machine.
4. Let the portion cool for 5 minutes.
5. Gently shake the can to eliminate the portion, and turn it out onto a rack to cool.

6 tablespoons margarine, at room
temperature 2 eggs, at room
temperature
½ cup coconut milk, at room temperature
½ cup pineapple juice, at room
temperature 1 cup sugar
1½ teaspoons coconut
extricate 2 cups generally
useful flour
¾ cup destroyed improved
coconut 1 teaspoon baking

powder

½ teaspoon salt

1. Place the margarine, eggs, coconut milk, pineapple juice, sugar, and coconut remove in your bread machine.
2. Program the machine for Quick cycle and press Start.
3. While the wet fixings are blending, mix together the flour, coconut, baking powder, and salt in a little bowl.
4. After the primary quick blending is done and the machine signals, add the dry ingredients.
5. When the portion is done, eliminate the can from the machine.
6. Let the portion cool for 5 minutes.
7. Gently shake the can to eliminate the portion, and turn it out onto a rack to cool.

Butter for lubing the can
1½ cups pumpkin purée
3 eggs, at room temperature
⅓ cup liquefied spread,
cooled 1 cup sugar
3 cups universally handy flour
1½ teaspoons baking powder
¾ teaspoon ground cinnamon
½ teaspoon baking soda
¼ teaspoon ground nutmeg
¼ teaspoon ground ginger
¼ teaspoon salt
Pinch ground
cloves

1. Lightly oil the bread can with butter.
2. Add the pumpkin, eggs, spread, and sugar.
3. Program the machine for Quick cycle and press Start.
4. Let the wet fixings be blended by the oars until the principal quick

Mixing cycle is done, around 10 minutes into the cycle.
5. While the wet fixings are blending, mix together the flour, baking powder, cinnamon, baking pop, nutmeg, ginger, salt, and cloves until well blended.
6. Add the dry fixings to the can when the subsequent quick Mixing cycle starts.
7. Scrape down the sides of the can once after the dry fixings are blended into the wet.
8. When the portion is done, eliminate the can from the machine.
9. Let the portion cool for 5 minutes.
10. Gently shake the can to eliminate the portion, and turn it out onto a rack to cool.

⅔ cup milk, at 80°F (27°C) to 90°F
(32°C) 1 tablespoon dissolved spread,
cooled
⅔ teaspoon minced
garlic 1 tablespoon sugar
⅔ teaspoon salt
2 cups white bread flour
¾ teaspoon bread machine or moment yeast
¼ cup slashed dark olives

1. Place the fixings in your bread machine as suggested by the manufacturer.
2. Set the machine to Basic cycle, select light or medium outside layer, and press Start.
3. When the portion is done, eliminate the can from the machine.
4. Let the portion cool for 5 minutes.
5. Gently shake the can to eliminate the portion, and turn it out onto a rack to cool.

½ cup water, at 80°F (27°C) to 90°F (32°C)
½ cup milk, at 80°F (27°C)
1½ tablespoons liquefied

margarine, cooled 3 tablespoons
honey
2 tablespoons
molasses 1½
teaspoons sugar
1 tablespoon skim milk powder
½ teaspoon salt
1½ cups entire wheat
flour 1 cup white bread
flour
2 teaspoons unsweetened cocoa powder
1 teaspoon bread machine or moment yeast
½ cup slashed dates

1. Place the fixings, with the exception of the dates, in your bread machine as suggested by the manufacturer.
2. Set the machine to Basic cycle, select light or medium outside, and press Start.
3. When the machine signals, add the hacked dates, or put them in the nut/raisin container and let the machine add them automatically.
4. When the portion is done, eliminate the can from the machine.
5. Let the portion cool for 5 minutes.
6. Gently shake the can to eliminate the portion, and turn it out onto a rack to cool.

⅔ cup milk, at 80°F (27°C) to 90°F
(32°C) 1⅔ tablespoons dissolved
margarine, cooled
4 teaspoons sugar
1 teaspoon salt
⅔ teaspoon ground cinnamon
Pinch ground cloves
2 cups white bread flour
1½ teaspoons bread machine or dynamic dry yeast

⅔ cup finely diced stripped apple

1. Place the fixings, aside from the apple, in your bread machine as suggested by the manufacturer.
2. Set the machine to Basic cycle, select light or medium hull, and press Start.
3. When the machine signals, add the apple to the can, or add it not long before the finish of the second Kneading cycle in the event that your machine doesn't have a signal.
4. When the portion is done, eliminate the can from the machine.
5. Let the portion cool for 5 minutes.
6. Gently shake the can to eliminate the portion, and turn it out onto a rack to cool.

½ cup plain yogurt, at room temperature
⅓ cup water, at 80°F (27°C) to 90°F
(32°C) 2 tablespoons honey
2 teaspoons dissolved spread,
cooled 1 teaspoon salt
⅓ teaspoon lemon
separate 1 teaspoon lime
zest
⅔ cup dried
blueberries 2 cups
white bread flour
1½ teaspoons bread machine or moment yeast

1. Place the fixings in your bread machine as suggested by the manufacturer.
2. Set the machine to Basic cycle, select light or medium outside layer, and press Start.
3. When the portion is done, eliminate the can from the machine.
4. Let the portion cool for 5 minutes.
5. Gently shake the can to eliminate the portion, and turn it out onto a rack to cool.

⅓ cup milk, at 80°F (27°C) to 90°F (32°C)
⅔ cup squashed banana
1 egg, at room temperature
1 tablespoon dissolved spread,
cooled 2 tablespoons honey
⅔ teaspoon unadulterated vanilla extract
⅓ teaspoon salt
⅔ cup entire wheat flour
¾ cup in addition to 1 tablespoon white
bread flour 1 teaspoon bread machine
or moment yeast

1. Place the fixings in your bread machine as suggested by the manufacturer.
2. Program the machine for Sweet bread and press Start.
3. When the portion is done, eliminate the can from the machine.
4. Let the portion cool for 5 minutes.
5. Gently shake the can to eliminate the portion, and turn it out onto a rack to cool.

¾ cup milk, at 80°F (27°C) to 90°F (32°C)
¾ cup sugar
⅔ cup softened margarine,
cooled 2 eggs, at room
temperature
¼ cup newly crushed squeezed orange, at room
temperature 1 tablespoon orange zest
1 teaspoon unadulterated
vanilla concentrate 2¼ cups
generally useful flour
1 cup improved dried
cranberries 1½ teaspoons
baking powder

½ teaspoon baking soda
½ teaspoon salt
¼ teaspoon ground nutmeg

1. Place the milk, sugar, margarine, eggs, squeezed orange, zing, and vanilla in your bread machine.
2. Program the machine for Quick cycle and press Start.
3. While the wet fixings are blending, mix together the flour, cranberries, baking powder, baking pop, salt, and nutmeg in a medium bowl.
4. After the main quick blending is done and the machine signals, add the dry ingredients.
5. When the portion is done, eliminate the can from the machine.
6. Let the portion cool for 5 minutes.
7. Gently shake the can to eliminate the portion, and turn it out onto a rack to cool.

¾ cup water, at 80°F (27°C) to 90°F
(32°C) 1½ tablespoons softened spread,
cooled
2 tablespoons sugar
½ teaspoon salt
½ teaspoon orange zest
¼ teaspoon ground
cinnamon Pinch ground
nutmeg
1¼ cups entire wheat flour
¾ cup white bread flour
1 teaspoon bread machine or moment yeast
¾ cup cleaved new plums

1. Place the fixings, with the exception of the plums, in your bread machine as suggested by the manufacturer.
2. Set the machine to Basic cycle, select light or medium covering, and press Start.

3. When the machine signals, add the hacked plums.
4. When the portion is done, eliminate the can from the machine.
5. Let the portion cool for 5 minutes.
6. Gently shake the can to eliminate the portion, and turn it out onto a rack to cool.

½ cup canned peaches, depleted and chopped
¼ cup weighty whipping cream, at 80°F (27°C) to 90°F (32°C) 1 egg, at room temperature
¾ tablespoon softened spread, cooled 1½ tablespoons sugar
¾ teaspoon salt
¼ teaspoon ground cinnamon
⅛ teaspoon ground nutmeg
¼ cup entire wheat flour 1¾ cups white bread flour
¾ teaspoons bread machine or moment yeast

1. Place the fixings in your bread machine as suggested by the manufacturer.
2. Set the machine to Basic cycle, select light or medium outside layer, and press Start.
3. When the portion is done, eliminate the can from the machine.
4. Let the portion cool for 5 minutes.
5. Gently shake the can to eliminate the portion, and turn it out onto a rack to cool.

1 cup plain Greek yogurt, at room temperature
½ cup milk, at room temperature
3 tablespoons margarine, at room temperature 2 eggs, at room temperature
½ cup sugar

¼ cup light brown sugar
1 teaspoon unadulterated vanilla extract
½ teaspoon lemon
zing 2 cups
universally handy
flour
1 tablespoon baking powder
¾ teaspoon salt
¼ teaspoon ground
nutmeg 1 cup blueberries

1. Place the yogurt, milk, spread, eggs, sugar, earthy colored sugar, vanilla, and zing in your bread machine.
2. Program the machine for Quick cycle and press Start.
3. While the wet fixings are blending, mix together the flour, baking powder, salt, and nutmeg in a medium bowl.
4. After the principal quick blending is done and the machine signals, add the dry ingredients.
5. When the subsequent Mixing cycle is finished, mix in the blueberries.
6. When the portion is done, eliminate the can from the machine.
7. Let the portion cool for 5 minutes.
8. Gently shake the can to eliminate the portion, and turn it out onto a rack to cool.

⅓ cup milk, at 80°F (27°C) to 90°F
(32°C) 1 egg, at room temperature
1½ tablespoons dissolved spread,
cooled 1 tablespoon honey
⅓ cup rolled oats
2 cups white bread flour
¾ teaspoon salt
1 teaspoon bread machine or moment yeast
⅓ cup dried blueberries

1. Place the fixings, with the exception of the blueberries, in your bread machine as suggested by the manufacturer.
2. Set the machine to Basic cycle, select light or medium outside, and press Start.
3. Add the blueberries when the machine signs or 5 minutes before the second Kneading cycle is finished.
4. When the portion is done, eliminate the can from the machine.
5. Let the portion cool for 5 minutes.
6. Gently shake the can to eliminate the portion, and turn it out onto a rack to cool.

Chapter 7: Nut and Seed Breads

Caraway Rye Bread

Makes 1 pound

¾ cup tepid water

1 tablespoon unsalted spread, diced 1 tablespoon molasses

½ cup rye flour

1 cup plain bread flour

½ cup entire wheat

flour 1 tablespoon milk

powder

¾ teaspoon salt

2 tablespoons earthy

colored sugar 1

tablespoon caraway

seeds

1¼ teaspoons moment dry yeast

1. Add the fixings into the bread machine according to the request for the fixings recorded above or adhere to your bread machine's guidance manual.

2. Select the Whole Wheat cycle and medium outside function.
3. When prepared, turn the bread out onto a drying rack and permit it to cool, then, at that point, serve.

1 tablespoon spread, mellowed
1½ tablespoons honey
¾ cup bread flour
⅔ cup entire wheat flour
½ teaspoon salt
½ teaspoon dynamic dry yeast
¼ cup flax seeds
¼ cup sunflower seeds

1. Place all fixings (with the exception of the sunflower seeds) into the bread machine, either in the request recorded, or as per your bread machine's guidance manual.
2. Select the Basic cycle, just as the delicate or medium outside layer function.
3. Just before your bread machine enters its last Kneading cycle (most machines will flag you with a blare around this time), add the sunflower seeds.
4. When prepared, turn the bread out onto a drying rack so it can cool, then, at that point, serve.

⅔ cup tepid water
1⅓ tablespoons olive oil
1⅓ tablespoons honey
1⅓ tablespoons molasses
1 teaspoon salt
⅔ cup entire wheat flour
1⅓ cups plain bread flour
1½ teaspoons dynamic dry yeast
¼ cup walnut nuts

¼ cup walnuts

1. Place all fixings (aside from the walnuts and pecans) into your bread machine, either in the request recorded, or as per the guidance manual that accompanied your bread machine.
2. Select the Basic cycle setting and pick the delicate outside layer work.
3. Before the last Kneading cycle, add your walnuts and walnuts.
4. When prepared, turn the bread out onto a drying rack so it can cool, then, at that point, serve.

½ cup milk, warmed

2 tablespoons unsalted

margarine 1½ cups plain

bread flour

½ cup multigrain cereal

¼ cup granulated brown sugar

¾ teaspoon salt

¾ teaspoon bread machine yeast

1. Add the fixings into the bread machine according to the request for the fixings recorded above or adhere to your bread machine's guidance manual.
2. Select the Basic cycle and medium covering function.
3. When prepared, turn the bread out onto a drying rack and permit it to cool, then, at that point, serve.

⅔ teaspoon salt

1 tablespoon and 1 teaspoon olive oil

⅔ cup entire wheat flour

1⅓ cups white bread

flour 1 teaspoon

dynamic dry yeast 2

teaspoons linseed

2 teaspoons pumpkin

seeds 2 teaspoons

sesame seeds 2 teaspoons poppy seeds

2 teaspoons sunflower seeds

1. Add all fixings to your bread machine in the specific request recorded. Seeds can be included any request, surprisingly long after the yeast.
2. Select the Basic cycle, alongside any outside work you desire.
3. When prepared, turn the bread out onto a drying rack so it can cool, then, at that point, serve.

½ tablespoon vegetable oil

½ teaspoon lemon juice 1 teaspoon salt

⅙ cup molasses

⅓ cup fast oatmeal

½ cup entire wheat flour 1⅓ cup plain bread flour 1½ cups walnuts

1½ teaspoons moment dry yeast

1. Add the fixings into the bread machine according to the request for the fixings recorded above or adhere to your bread machine's guidance manual.
2. Select the Basic cycle and delicate hull function.
3. When prepared, turn the bread out onto a drying rack and permit it to cool, then, at that point, serve.

⅔ cup tepid water

1 tablespoon vegetable oil 1⅓ tablespoons honey

¼ teaspoon salt

½ cup rolled oats

½ cup entire wheat flour

½ cup bread flour
1 teaspoon dynamic dry yeast
⅓ cup dates, cleaved and pitted
⅓ cup almonds, chopped

1. Add all fixings (aside from the dates and almonds) to the bread machine, either in the request recorded, or as per your bread machine's guidance manual.
2. Select the nut and raisin setting, just as the delicate covering function.
3. Just before your bread machine enters its last Kneading cycle (most machines will flag you with a blare around this time), add the dates and almonds.
4. When prepared, turn the bread out onto a drying rack so it can cool, then, at that point, serve.

1 cup in addition to 2 tablespoons
without fat milk 1 egg yolk
1 teaspoon almond extract
1 (1-pound/454-g) box white bread machine mix
½ cup slashed fragmented whitened almonds
⅓ cup currants
1 tablespoon poppy seeds
1 tablespoon light earthy
colored sugar 2 teaspoons
gluten
1 yeast parcel (remembered for mix)

1. Place every one of the fixings in the container as indicated by the request in the maker's directions. Set the covering for medium and program for the Basic cycle; press Start.
2. When the baking cycle closes, promptly eliminate the bread from the dish and spot it on a rack. Let cool to room temperature before slicing.

1 cup in addition to 2 tablespoons water

1 (1-pound/454-g) box white bread machine blend 2 teaspoons gluten
1 yeast parcel (remembered for mix)
¾ cup hacked dried figs
¼ cup cleaved walnuts

1. Place the fixings, with the exception of the figs and pecans, in the dish as indicated by the request in the maker's guidelines. Set the outside layer for dim and program for the Basic or Fruit and Nut cycle; press Start. At the point when the machine blares, or between Knead 1 and Knead 2, add the figs and walnuts.
2. When the baking cycle closes, promptly eliminate the bread from the skillet and spot it on a rack. Let cool to room temperature before slicing.

1¼ cups walnut parts 1½ cups water
1½ tablespoons margarine, cut into pieces 3⅓ cups bread flour
⅔ cup dim rye flour
1½ tablespoons dull brown sugar
1 tablespoon in addition to 2 teaspoons gluten
2 teaspoons salt
2½ teaspoons SAF yeast or 1 tablespoon bread machine yeast
½ cup dim raisins

1. Preheat the stove to 350°F (180°C).
2. Spread the nuts on a baking sheet. Prepare for 10 minutes, mixing two times. Cool on the baking sheet. Hack the nuts into huge pieces and set aside.
3. Place the fixings, with the exception of the nuts and the raisins, in the dish as indicated by the request in the producer's guidelines. Set covering on medium and program for the Basic or Fruit and Nut cycle; press Start. At the point when the machine blares, or between Knead 1 and Knead 2, add the nuts and the raisins.

4. When the baking cycle closes, quickly eliminate the bread from the container and spot it on a rack. Let cool to room temperature before slicing.

⅔ cup water
⅔ cup dry white wine
⅓ cup olive oil
2⅔ cups bread flour
1 cup entire wheat flour
⅓ cup rye flour
1 tablespoon in addition to 1 teaspoon gluten
1 tablespoon in addition to 2 teaspoons sugar
2 teaspoons salt
2½ teaspoons SAF yeast or 1 tablespoon bread machine yeast
½ cup pine nuts, coarsely chopped

1. Place the fixings, aside from the pine nuts, in the skillet as per the request in the producer's guidelines. Set outside on medium and program for the Basic or French cycle; press Start. Five minutes into Knead 2, sprinkle in the pine nuts.
2. When the baking cycle closes, promptly eliminate the bread from the skillet and spot it on a rack. Let cool to room temperature before slicing.

1⅓ cups
buttermilk 1 huge
egg
3 tablespoons sunflower seed
oil 2½ cups bread flour
1 cup entire wheat flour
½ cup cornmeal
⅔ cup crude sunflower seeds
3 tablespoons dim earthy
colored sugar 2 tablespoons
gluten

2 teaspoons salt

2½ teaspoons SAF yeast or 1 tablespoon bread machine yeast

1. Place every one of the fixings in the dish as per the request in the producer's directions. Set hull on dull and program for the Whole Wheat cycle; press Start.
2. When the baking cycle closes, promptly eliminate the bread from the skillet and spot it on a rack. Let cool to room temperature before slicing.

⅔ cup squeezed

orange 1 cup sans

fat milk

4 tablespoons margarine, cut into

pieces 3½ cups bread flour

½ cup entire wheat flour

⅓ cup light brown sugar

1 tablespoon in addition to 1 teaspoon gluten

2 teaspoons cumin seed, squashed in a mortar and

pestle 2 teaspoons salt

2¼ teaspoons SAF yeast or 2¾ teaspoons bread machine yeast

1. Place every one of the fixings in the container as indicated by the request in the producer's directions. Set outside layer on dull and program for the Basic cycle; press Start. The batter ball will be firm and smooth, yet springy.
2. When the baking cycle closes, quickly eliminate the bread from the skillet and spot it on a rack. Let cool to room temperature before slicing.

1½ cups water

3⅓ cups bread flour

⅔ cup entire wheat flour

1 tablespoon sesame

seeds 1 tablespoon

aniseeds

2½ teaspoons salt

2½ teaspoons SAF yeast or 1 tablespoon bread machine yeast 2 tablespoons yellow cornmeal, for sprinkling

1. Place all the batter fixings in the container as per the request in the maker's directions. Program for the Dough cycle; press Start.
2. Turn the mixture out onto a work surface and gap it into 2 equivalent segments. Manipulate each part into a ball and let rest for 10 minutes covered with a perfect tea towel. With your fingers, dampen the outer layer of every mixture ball with some olive oil; press with your palm to straighten each into a circle 1 inch thick and 6 crawls in width. Dust the work surface with a touch of flour to hold the mixture back from adhering to it and cover the circles with the towel. Let rest for 1½ to 2 hours, until puffy. Prick the outer layer of each portion with the prongs of a fork to tenderly delivery the gas.
3. Preheat the stove to 400°F (205°C). Sprinkle a baking sheet with cornmeal and spot the portions on the baking sheet.
4. Immediately place the portions in the stove (it will not be up to temperature or hot yet) and prepare for precisely 12 minutes. Lessen the broiler temperature to 300°F (150°C) and heat for an extra 35 to 40 minutes, or until the breads are brown and sound empty when tapped on the base with your finger. Eliminate to a rack to cool prior to slicing into wedges to serve.

1⅔ cups warm water

3 tablespoons moment potato

drops 2 tablespoons margarine or lard

3½ cups bread flour

½ cup potato starch

flour 2 tablespoons sugar

1 tablespoon gluten

1 tablespoon caraway seeds 2 teaspoons salt

2 teaspoons SAF yeast or 2½ teaspoons bread machine yeast

1. Place the moment potato chips in the water in a bowl. Let represent 5 minutes. The chips will grow and mellow, and the water become cloudy.
2. Place the fixings in the container as per the request in the producer's guidelines, adding the potato water with the margarine or grease as the fluid fixings. Set outside on dim and program for the Quick Yeast Bread or Rapid cycle; press Start. The batter ball will be smooth and delicate. Assuming the batter rises more than 66% of the way up the container, tenderly empty the mixture a piece. This will hold the batter back from hitting the window during baking.
3. When the baking cycle closes, quickly eliminate the bread from the container and spot it on a rack. Let cool to room temperature before slicing.

Chapter 8: Specialty Flour Breads
Honey Cornmeal Bread
Makes 2 pounds

1½ cups water
2 tablespoons unsalted margarine cut into pieces
¼ cup honey
3½ cups bread flour
½ cup yellow cornmeal
½ cup dry buttermilk powder
1 tablespoon in addition to 2
teaspoons gluten 1½ teaspoons
salt
2½ teaspoons SAF yeast or 1 tablespoon bread machine yeast

1. Place every one of the fixings in the skillet as per the request in the maker's guidelines. Set covering on dim and program for the Basic cycle; press Start.
2. When the baking cycle closes, quickly eliminate the bread from the

container and spot it on a rack. Let cool to room temperature before slicing.

⅔ cup milk
⅔ cup water
3 tablespoons olive oil
4 cups bread flour
⅔ cup yellow cornmeal
3 tablespoons sugar
2 tablespoons gluten
2 teaspoons salt
2½ teaspoons SAF yeast or 1 tablespoon bread machine yeast
1½ cups canned hominy, rinsed

1. Place every one of the fixings, with the exception of the hominy, in the dish as per the request in the maker's guidelines. Set hull on dim and program for the Basic or Fruit and Nut cycle; press Start. At the point when the machine blares, or between Knead 1 and Knead 2, add the hominy.
2. When the baking cycle closes, quickly eliminate the bread from the dish and spot it on a rack. Let cool to room temperature before slicing.

1½ cups water
¼ cup honey
3 tablespoons sunflower seed oil
3¼ cups bread flour
¾ cup entire wheat flour
⅓ cup polenta
¼ cup entire crude millet
¼ cup crude sunflower seeds
2 tablespoons gluten
2 teaspoons salt

2½ teaspoons SAF yeast or 1 tablespoon bread machine yeast

1. Place every one of the fixings in the container as indicated by the request in the producer's directions. Set outside layer on medium and program for the Basic or Whole Wheat cycle; press Start.
2. When the baking cycle closes, quickly eliminate the bread from the container and spot it on a rack. Let cool to room temperature before slicing.

1⅓ cups
buttermilk 1 huge
egg
3 tablespoons unsalted margarine, cut into
pieces 3 cups bread flour
1 cup entire wheat flour
½ cup light buckwheat flour
3 tablespoons dim earthy
colored sugar Grated zing of
1 enormous orange
1 tablespoon in addition to 1 teaspoon gluten
2 teaspoons salt
2½ teaspoons SAF yeast or 1 tablespoon bread machine yeast

1. Place every one of the fixings in the container as per the request in the producer's directions. Set hull on dull and program for the Basic cycle; press Start. The batter ball will be damp and springy.
2. When the baking cycle closes, promptly eliminate the bread from the skillet and spot it on a rack. Let cool to room temperature before slicing.

1½ cups water
2 tablespoons unsalted spread, cut into
pieces 3 tablespoons dull honey
3½ cups bread flour
½ cup light buckwheat flour

½ cup entire millet

1 tablespoon in addition to 1 teaspoon gluten

2 teaspoons salt

2½ teaspoons SAF yeast or 1 tablespoon bread machine yeast

1. Place every one of the fixings in the dish as indicated by the request in the producer's directions. Set covering on dim and program for the Basic cycle; press Start.
2. When the baking cycle closes, quickly eliminate the bread from the container and spot it on a rack. Let cool to room temperature before slicing.

1⅛ cups without

fat milk 1 huge egg

4 tablespoons spread or margarine, cut into

pieces 3¼ cups bread flour

¾ cup chestnut flour

3 tablespoons dull earthy

colored sugar 3 tablespoons

minced pecans

1 tablespoon in addition to 1 teaspoon gluten

2 teaspoons salt

2½ teaspoons SAF yeast or 1 tablespoon bread machine yeast

1. Place every one of the fixings in the skillet as per the request in the maker's directions. Set outside on medium or dull and program for the Basic cycle; press Start. The batter ball will be clammy and springy.
2. When the baking cycle closes, quickly eliminate the bread from the container and spot it on a rack. Let cool to room temperature before slicing.

1⅓ cups buttermilk

¼ cup dim honey

¼ cup olive oil

3 cups bread flour

¾ cup chestnut flour

½ cup polenta

2 tablespoons gluten

2 teaspoons salt

2¾ teaspoons SAF yeast or 1 tablespoon in addition to ¼ teaspoon bread machine yeast

1. Place every one of the fixings in the container as indicated by the request in the maker's directions. Set outside layer on dim and program for the Basic cycle; press Start. The mixture ball will be firm, yet marginally sticky.
2. 2 When the baking cycle closes, promptly eliminate the bread from the dish and spot it on a rack. Let cool to room temperature before slicing.

1½ cups water

3 tablespoons light earthy colored sugar 3 tablespoons vegetable oil

3 cups bread flour

⅔ cup grain flour

⅓ cup entire wheat flour

¼ cup dry buttermilk powder 2 tablespoons gluten

1½ teaspoons ground cinnamon 2 teaspoons salt

2½ teaspoons SAF yeast or 1 tablespoon bread machine yeast

1. Place every one of the fixings in the skillet as per the request in the maker's guidelines. Set covering on medium and program for the Basic or Whole Wheat cycle; press Start.
2. When the baking cycle closes, quickly eliminate the bread from the container and spot it on a rack. Let cool to room temperature

before slicing.

3 tablespoons canola oil
3 tablespoons honey
3 tablespoons dull earthy colored sugar
1 enormous egg
2 cups entire wheat flour
1½ cups bread flour
½ cup full-fat soy flour
2 tablespoons wheat germ
⅓ cup nonfat dry milk
2 tablespoons gluten
2 teaspoons salt
1 tablespoon SAF yeast or 1 tablespoon in addition to ½ teaspoon bread machine yeast

1. Place the fixings in the skillet as indicated by the request in the producer's directions. Set hull on dim and program for the Whole Wheat cycle; press Start.
2. When the baking cycle closes, promptly eliminate the bread from the container and spot it on a rack. Let cool to room temperature before slicing.

3¼ cups bread flour
¾ cup ivory or dull teff flour
1 tablespoon in addition to 2 teaspoons gluten
2 teaspoons salt
1 tablespoon SAF yeast or 1 tablespoon in addition to ½ teaspoon bread machine yeast

1. Place every one of the fixings in the dish as indicated by the request in the maker's guidelines. Set outside layer on dim and program for the Basic cycle; press Start.

2. When the baking cycle closes, promptly eliminate the bread from the skillet and spot it on a rack. Let cool to room temperature before slicing.

Chapter 9: Jams, Preserves, and Chutneys

Strawberry Jam

Makes 2½ cups

1 pound (454 g) new strawberries, washed, depleted, and hulled 1 tablespoon new lemon juice
¾ (2-ounce/57-g) box powdered natural product gelatin 1 cup sugar, or to taste

1. Coarsely smash the berries with a potato masher, or put them in a food processor and heartbeat a couple of times, leaving a couple of entire berries or pieces. You will have around 2½ cups. Place the organic product in the bread container. Add the lemon squeeze and sprinkle with the gelatin. Let represent 10 minutes. Add the sugar.
2. Program the machine for the Jam cycle and press Start. At the point when the machine signals toward the finish of the cycle, cautiously eliminate the container with weighty stove gloves. You can scratch the jam into heat-safe containers immediately, utilizing an elastic spatula. For different containers, let the jam sit in the search for gold minutes prior to moving. Let remain until cool. Cover and store in the fridge for as long as 2 months, or spoon into little cooler sacks and freeze.

1 pound (454 g) new blueberries, rinsed
½ (2-ounce/57-g) box powdered organic product gelatin 1½ cups sugar, or to taste
3 tablespoons crème de cassis alcohol 2 tablespoons new lemon juice

1. Combine every one of the fixings in the bread skillet. Let represent

15 minutes to disintegrate the sugar.

2. Program the machine for the Jam cycle and press Start. At the point when the machine blares toward the finish of the cycle, cautiously eliminate the skillet with weighty stove gloves. You can scratch the jam into heat-safe containers immediately, utilizing an elastic spatula. For different containers, let the jam sit in the prospect minutes prior to moving. Let remain until cool. Store, covered, in the cooler for as long as 2 months, or spoon into little cooler packs and freeze.

3 cups new raspberries, rinsed
½ (2-ounce/57-g) box powdered organic
product gelatin 1¾ cups sugar, or to taste
3 tablespoons new lemon juice

1. Combine every one of the fixings in the bread container. Let represent 15 minutes to disintegrate the sugar.
2. Program the machine for the Jam cycle and press Start. At the point when the machine signals toward the finish of the cycle, cautiously eliminate the container with weighty broiler gloves. You can scratch the jam into heat-safe containers immediately, utilizing an elastic spatula. For different containers, let the jam sit in the prospect minutes prior to moving. Let remain until cool. Store, covered, in the fridge for as long as 2 months, or spoon into little cooler sacks and freeze.

2½ cups new boysenberries, rinsed
1 (2-ounce/57-g) box powdered organic
product gelatin 1 cup sugar, or to taste
2 tablespoons new lemon juice

1. Combine every one of the fixings in the bread dish. Let represent 15 minutes to break down the sugar.
2. Program the machine for the Jam cycle and press Start. At the point when the machine signals toward the finish of the cycle, cautiously eliminate the skillet with weighty stove gloves. You can scratch the jam into heat-safe containers immediately, utilizing an elastic spatula. For different containers, let the jam sit in the search

for gold minutes prior to moving. Let remain until cool. Store, covered, in the cooler for as long as 2 months, or spoon into little cooler packs and freeze.

1 pound (454 g) pitted crisp Bing cherries (you will have both entire cherries and pieces after the pitting)

1 cup sugar, or to taste

1 tablespoon new lemon

juice Pinch of salt

1½ tablespoons powdered organic product pectin

1. Combine the cherries, sugar, lemon squeeze, and salt in the bread skillet. Let represent 15 minutes to disintegrate the sugar. Sprinkle with the pectin.
2. Program the machine for the Jam cycle and press Start. At the point when the machine blares toward the finish of the cycle, cautiously eliminate the skillet with weighty broiler gloves. You can scratch the jam into heat-safe containers immediately, utilizing an elastic spatula. For different containers, let the jam sit in the search for gold minutes prior to moving. Let remain until cool. Store, covered, in the cooler for as long as 2 months, or spoon into little cooler packs and freeze.

3 to 4 huge peaches (around 1 pound/454

g) 1 cup sugar, or to taste

2 tablespoons new lemon juice

1 (2-ounce/57-g) box powdered natural product pectin

1. Peel and pit the peaches. Coarsely pulverize by hand with a potato masher, or heartbeat a couple of times in the food processor. You will have around 2½ cups.
2. Combine the peaches, sugar, and lemon juice in the bread container. Let represent 30 minutes to break down the sugar. Sprinkle with the gelatin.
3. Program the machine for the Jam cycle and press Start. At the point when the machine signals toward the finish of the cycle, cautiously eliminate the skillet with weighty broiler gloves. You

can scratch the jam into heat-safe containers immediately, utilizing an elastic spatula. For different containers, let the jam sit in the prospect minutes prior to moving. Let remain until cool. Store, covered, in the fridge for as long as 2 months, or spoon into little cooler sacks and freeze.

2 cups hollowed and cleaved new
apricots 1 tablespoon new lemon
juice
½ (2-ounce/57-g) box powdered organic
product gelatin 1¼ cups sugar, or to taste

1. Place the apricots and the lemon juice in the bread container. Sprinkle with the gelatin. Let represent 10 minutes. Add the sugar.
2. Program the machine for the Jam cycle and press Start. At the point when the machine blares toward the finish of the cycle, cautiously eliminate the skillet with weighty stove gloves. You can scratch the jam into heat-safe containers immediately, utilizing an elastic spatula. For different containers, let the jam sit in the search for gold minutes prior to moving. Let remain until cool. Store, covered, in the fridge for as long as about a month and a half, or spoon into little cooler packs and freeze.

4 enormous kiwi (1 pound/454 g), stripped, cut, and coarsely
hacked 2 tablespoons finely julienned lemon zest
3 tablespoons new lemon juice
1½ tablespoons powdered natural
product gelatin 1½ cups sugar

1. Combine every one of the fixings in the bread skillet. Let represent 20 minutes to break up the sugar.
2. Program the machine for the Jam cycle and press Start. At the point when the machine blares toward the finish of the cycle, cautiously eliminate the skillet with weighty stove gloves. You can scratch the jam into heat-safe containers immediately, utilizing an elastic spatula. For different containers, let the jam sit in the prospect minutes prior to moving. Let remain until cool. Store,

covered, in the cooler for as long as 2 months, or spoon into little cooler packs and freeze.

1 pound (454 g) rhubarb stalks, cut about ½ inch thick
1½ cups sugar
½ (2-ounce/57-g) box powdered organic product pectin
¼ cup hacked dried apricots

1. Mix the rhubarb with the sugar in a glass bowl, cover freely with cling wrap, and let remain at room temperature for 12 hours.
2. Combine the rhubarb-sugar blend, the gelatin, and the apricots in the bread pan.
3. Program the machine for the Jam cycle and press Start. At the point when the machine signals toward the finish of the cycle, cautiously eliminate the dish with weighty stove gloves. You can scratch the jam into heat-safe containers immediately, utilizing an elastic spatula. For different containers, let the jam sit in the search for gold minutes prior to moving. Let remain until cool. Store, covered, in the fridge for as long as 3 weeks, or spoon into little cooler packs and freeze.

¼ pound (113 g) dried apple rings,
slashed 1¼ cups unsweetened, unfiltered
squeezed apple 2 tablespoons apple juice
vinegar
1½ teaspoons ground cinnamon
½ teaspoon ground allspice
½ teaspoon ground cloves

1. Combine every one of the fixings in the bread container. Let remain at room temperature for 1 hour to mellow the apples.
2. Program the machine for the Jam cycle and press Start. At the point when the machine blares toward the finish of the cycle, cautiously eliminate the skillet with weighty stove gloves and let cool until warm.
3. Using an elastic spatula, scratch the combination into a food processor fitted with the metal cutting edge and interaction until

smooth. Scratch the creamy fruit spread into a glass container. Let remain at room temperature until cool. Store, covered, in the fridge for up to 2 months.

1 (15-ounce/425-g) can pumpkin purée
¾ cup stripped, cored, and coarsely ground new Pippin, Granny Smith, or other firm, tart cooking apple
½ cup unsweetened, unfiltered apple juice
½ cup light brown sugar
½ teaspoon ground cinnamon
½ teaspoon ground nutmeg
½ teaspoon ground cloves
3 tablespoons unsalted butter

1. Combine every one of the fixings in the bread pan.
2. Program the machine for the Jam cycle and press Start. At the point when the machine blares toward the finish of the cycle, cautiously eliminate the container with weighty broiler gloves. Mix in the spread until it liquefies. You can scratch the natural product margarine into heat-safe containers immediately, utilizing an elastic spatula. For different containers, let the natural product margarine sit in the search for gold minutes prior to moving. Let remain until cool. Store, covered, in the cooler for as long as 2 months, or spoon into little cooler sacks and freeze.

1 (28-ounce/794-g) can tomato
purée 1 little yellow onion, cut into
pieces 1 huge shallot, chopped
1 clove garlic, pressed
½ cup apple juice vinegar
⅓ cup water
¼ cup light brown sugar
1 teaspoon ground
allspice Pinch of ground
cinnamon Pinch of
ground cloves Pinch of

ground mace Pinch of
ground ginger
Pinch of Coleman's dry mustard
Pinch of squashed hot red pepper
drops Fresh-ground dark pepper
Sea salt

1. In a food processor, ideally, or in clusters in a blender, join the tomato purée, onion, shallot, and garlic. Process until just smooth.
2. Pour the tomato combination into the bread container. Add the vinegar, water, sugar, and spices.
3. Program the machine for the Jam cycle and press Start. At the point when the machine signals toward the finish of the cycle, the ketchup will have diminished marginally and thickened. Add salt and pepper to taste. Cautiously eliminate the skillet with weighty stove gloves. You can scratch the ketchup into heat-safe containers immediately, utilizing an elastic spatula. For different containers, let the ketchup sit in the prospect minutes prior to moving. Serve warm, room temperature, or chilled. Store canvassed in the fridge for up to 2 months.

Makes 2 cups

2 new firm-ready mangoes (around 1½ pounds/680 g)
¼ cup dull or brilliant raisins,
cleaved 1 medium shallot, minced
½ cup dim brown sugar
An inadequate tablespoon of minced
new ginger 2 teaspoons hot pepper
flakes
Pinch of ground cloves
⅛ teaspoon salt
½ cup apple juice vinegar
2 tablespoons new lime juice

1. Peel the mango by standing the organic product stem (more

extensive) end up. Make 4 vertical cuts, through the skin, to score the slight hard skin and gap the natural product into quarters longwise. Beginning at the top, strip the skin back from each quarter, very much like a banana. Cut the tissue away from the level seed in strips. Coarsely slash. You will have around 2 cups.

2. Combine every one of the fixings in the bread pan.
3. Program the machine for the Jam cycle and press start. At the point when the machine signals toward the finish of the cycle, cautiously eliminate the skillet with weighty stove gloves. You can scratch the chutney into heat-safe containers immediately, utilizing an elastic spatula. For different containers, let the chutney sit in the search for gold minutes prior to moving. Let remain until cool. Store, covered, in the fridge for as long as 2 months. Serve at room temperature.

Makes 1¾ cups

3 to 4 new peaches (around 1 pound/454 g) or 1 pound (454 g) frozen unsweetened peach cuts, defrosted

Piece of new ginger root around 3 inches long

⅓ cup brilliant raisins, chopped

2 little white bubbling onions,

minced 1 little clove garlic,

minced

¾ cup dim earthy

colored sugar 2

teaspoons bean stew

powder

2 teaspoons yellow mustard seeds

¼ teaspoon salt

½ cup apple juice vinegar

1. Peel the peaches by plunging them momentarily into a dish of bubbling water to slacken the skins. Promptly cool them by holding them under chilly water, and the skins will sneak off. Coarsely hack the peaches and spot them in the bread pan.
2. Peel and mince the ginger so you have around 2½ tablespoons.

You can utilize somewhat more or somewhat less, contingent upon how hot you need the chutney. Consolidate the ginger and every one of the excess fixings with the peaches in the bread pan.

3. Program the machine for the Jam cycle and press start. At the point when the machine blares toward the finish of the cycle, cautiously eliminate the container with weighty stove gloves. You can scratch the chutney into heat-safe containers immediately, utilizing an elastic spatula. For different containers, let the chutney sit in the search for gold minutes prior to moving. Let remain until cool. Store, covered, in the fridge for as long as 2 months. Serve at room temperature.

Makes 2 cups

2 medium tart cooking apples, stripped, cored, and finely chopped
⅔ cup dim brown sugar
⅓ cup finely cleaved dried apricots
⅓ cup finely hacked dried pineapple or dried pears
⅓ cup dull or brilliant raisins
¼ cup finely slashed red chime pepper
Piece of new ginger root around 1 inch since a long time
ago, stripped and ground 1 enormous shallot, finely
chopped
1 clove garlic, pressed
¼ teaspoon ground cayenne
pepper Pinch of hot pepper
flakes
Pinch of ground turmeric or curry powder
½ teaspoon salt
⅔ cup apple juice vinegar

1. Combine every one of the fixings in the bread pan.
2. Program the machine for the Jam cycle and press Start. At the point when the machine signals toward the finish of the cycle, cautiously eliminate the skillet with weighty broiler gloves. You can scratch the chutney into heat-safe containers immediately, utilizing an elastic spatula. For different containers, let the chutney

sit in the search for gold minutes prior to moving. Let remain until cool. Store, covered, in the cooler, for as long as 2 months. Serve at room temperature.

Appendix 1 Measurement Conversion Chart

VOLUME EQUIVALENTS (DRY)

US STANDARD	METRIC (APPROXIMATE)
1/8 teaspoon	0.5 mL
1/4 teaspoon	1 mL
1/2 teaspoon	2 mL
3/4 teaspoon	4 mL
1 teaspoon	5 mL
1 tablespoon	15 mL
1/4 cup	59 mL
1/2 cup	118 mL
3/4 cup	177 mL
1 cup	235 mL
2 cups	475 mL
3 cups	700 mL
4 cups	1 L

VOLUME EQUIVALENTS (LIQUID)

US STANDARD	US STANDARD (OUNCES)	METRIC (APPROXIMATE)
2 tablespoons	1 fl.oz.	30 mL
1/4 cup	2 fl.oz.	60 mL
1/2 cup	4 fl.oz.	120 mL
1 cup	8 fl.oz.	240 mL
1 1/2 cup	12 fl.oz.	355 mL
2 cups or 1 pint	16 fl.oz.	475 mL
4 cups or 1 quart	32 fl.oz.	1 L
1 gallon	128 fl.oz.	4 L

TEMPERATURES EQUIVALENTS

FAHRENHEIT (F)	CELSIUS (C) (APPROXIMATE)
225 °F	107 °C
250 °F	120 °C
275 °F	135 °C
300 °F	150 °C
325 °F	160 °C
350 °F	180 °C
375 °F	190 °C
400 °F	205 °C
425 °F	220 °C
450 °F	235 °C
475 °F	245 °C
500 °F	260 °C

WEIGHT EQUIVALENTS

US STANDARD	METRIC (APPROXIMATE)
1 ounce	28 g
2 ounces	57 g
5 ounces	142 g
10 ounces	284 g
15 ounces	425 g
16 ounces (1 pound)	455 g
1.5 pounds	680 g
2 pounds	907 g

www.ingramcontent.com/pod-product-compliance
Lightning Source LLC
LaVergne TN
LVHW041554131224
799037LV00026B/247